Analog Hunger in a Digital World

Other Books of Interest from St. Augustine's Press

Zbigniew Janowski, *Homo Americanus:*
The Rise of Totalitarian Democracy in America

Predrag Cicovacki, *The Ethic of the Upward Gaze:*
Essays Inspired by Immanuel Kant and Nicolai Hartmann

Leo Strauss, *Leo Strauss' Published but Uncollected English Writings*

Michael Davis, *Electras: Aeschylus, Sophocles, and Euripides*

D. Q. McInerny, *Being Philosophical*

Gabriel Marcel, *Toward Another Kingdom: Two Dramas of the Darker Years*

Gabriel Marcel, *The Invisible Threshold: Two Plays by Gabriel Marcel*

D. C. Schindler, *God and the City*

Gene Fendt, *Camus' Plague: Myth for Our World*

Roger Scruton, *The Politics of Culture and Other Essays*

Nalin Ranasinghe, *Shakespeare's Reformation:*
Christian Humanism and the Death of God

Francisco Insa, *The Formation of Affectivity: A Christian Approach*

Daniel J. Mahoney, *Recovering Politics, Civilization, and the Soul:*
Essays on Pierre Manent and Roger Scruton

Pierre Manent, *The Religion of Humanity: The Illusion of Our Times*

Stanley Rosen, *The Language of Love: An Interpretation of Plato's Phaedrus*

James M. Rhodes, *Knowledge, Sophistry, and Scientific Politics:*
Plato's Dialogues Theaetetus, Sophist, and Statesman

Michael Franz (editor), *Eric Voegelin's Late Meditations and Essays:*
Critical Commentary Companions

John von Heyking, *Comprehensive Judgment and Absolute Selflessness:*
Winston Churchill on Politics as Friendship

Winston Churchill, *Savrola*

Winston Churchill, *The River War*

Winston Churchill, *My Early Life*

Analog Hunger
in a Digital World

Confronting Today's Identity Crisis

PAUL C. VITZ

ST. AUGUSTINE'S PRESS

South Bend, Indiana

Manufactured in the United States of America.

1 2 3 4 5 6 29 28 27 26 25 24

Library of Congress Control Number: 2024940215

Paperback ISBN: 978-1-58731-053-9
ebook ISBN: 978-1-58731-054-6

∞ The paper used in this publication meets the minimum
requirements of the American National Standard for Information Sciences –
Permanence of Paper for Printed Materials, ANSI Z39.48-1984.

St. Augustine's Press
www.staugustine.net

This book is dedicated to my wife and family. Through the many, many years during which I brought up the topic of analog and digital they wisely suggested many ideas and patiently endured the topic when it no longer really interested them. Many thanks.

TABLE OF CONTENTS

ACKNOWLEDGEMENTS

Numerous people have contributes to the various drafts of this book. I would like to especially thank Fr. Lary Kutz, Tracy Mehan, Pat Fagan and Anne Needham for their important contributions. In addition, I would like to thank Iain McGilchrist whom I have never met or communicated with but I have found his writings as very especially helpful.

FOREWORD

Most of us already know that we are living in a period of crisis. I am not thinking of military and economic crises, although they are quite real, but rather of a crisis of personal meaning and identity. Why is this happening?

For centuries—and especially in the past hundred years or so—we have believed in progress. We have thought that the introduction of new machines and technology would make us happier. Here in the United States this freedom from many mundane tasks, facilitated by new technology, has become commonplace for millions of people. Yet, strangely, today we find ourselves less happy than our parents or grandparents, whose lives seem to have been more restricted. In the United States, measures of longevity have begun to show long-term decline, while evidence of suicide, addiction, and drug overdoses show long-term increases. Even worse has been the growth of anxiety, depression, loneliness, and identity disorders, especially among the young.[1,2]

Because of these negative trends it should not seem surprising that our present culture is filled with many who are searching for meaning, especially in the form of identity. Most often this search shows up in what is known as identity politics. Being an "American" is seen as an abstraction, and now we look to much more specific aspects of ourselves to give us meaning—such as race, ethnicity, and sexual identity. But the rather new and intense search for identity shows up in many other often strange ways, which will be treated in some detail later.

In this book, I start with the assumption that the link between increasing technology and positive progress, as shown by a general increase in happiness and well-being, has come to an end. Perhaps such a link might be re-established in the future, but it seems clear that at present, technology is not leading us to a genuine and fulfilling progress.

The conflict between the technological understanding of progress and the present widespread anxiety shows itself most clearly in the many movies

1

and novels predicting a disastrous technological future. Probably the first such critique is the still well-known novel *Frankenstein* (1818) by Mary Shelly. Curiously, Winston Churchill, some ninety years ago, expressed a deep concern about an anti-human technological future when he wrote:

> Science is the cause. Her once feeble vanguards ... have now become a vast organized united class-conscious army marching forward upon all the fronts towards objectives none may measure or define. It is a proud, ambitious army which cares nothing for all the laws that men have made; nothing for their most time-honoured customs, or most dearly cherished beliefs, or deepest instincts.
>
> It is therefore above all things important that the moral philosophy and spiritual conceptions of men and nations should hold their own amid these formidable scientific evolutions. It would be much better to call a halt in material progress and discovery rather than to be mastered by our own apparatus and the forces which it directs.... Without an equal growth of Mercy, Pity, Peace and Love, Science herself may destroy all that makes human life majestic and tolerable.[3]

Equally telling are the important critiques of our technological society by serious thinkers over the years, which by now have become common. Important examples include, among many, Aldous Huxley, Jacques Ellul, Jurgen Habermas, Wendell Berry, Robert Bellah, Charles Taylor, Neil Postman, and Martin Rees.[4]

More recently, I think that Charles Taylor got the general problem well summarized some thirty years ago.[5] He listed three social pathologies that were undermining American society with unfortunate consequences for all:

1. Our social freedom has been gotten at the cost of "older moral horizons" and social hierarchies. The result has been a disenchanted "individualism" focused on the self, which flattens and narrows our lives, making them less meaningful and less concerned with others.
2. We now have "primacy of instrumental reason" with no basis for any moral evaluation beyond maximum efficiency. This results in a

technological society that has destroyed the language of moral ends and has reduced human relations to a commodity to be bought and sold, creating anxiety in the face of revolutionary technological development.

3. From the preceding two predicaments there has come a political pathology, namely the loss of genuine social, and even political, freedom to the soft despotism of a bureaucratic state as the individual finds himself unable to maintain an identity against the prevailing opinions and social forces.[6]

Taylor clearly identifies the loss of meaning and morality, fear of technology, and loss of freedom to government systems. Added on in the thirty years since Taylor wrote has been the loss of privacy and personal freedom to systems on the internet that now monitor emails and other personal communications. Even fifty years ago, no government or outside system knew or had a record of what we said in our personal interactions.

Making my case here, however, for the *special digital way* in which technology is destroying our well-being will require some new vocabulary and a modest amount of brain work, work that I believe will be worth it and often, I hope, simply fun. I will also be making the case that *analog experience* is the only reliable source of meaning in our life and that its loss has led to the growth in meaninglessness and especially to the loss of personal identity.

For this book, I believe I have two major, somewhat independent, audiences: those who know about digital things and those who are concerned with our present cultural and identity crisis. Since I am going to show how these two audiences are related, I hope each will be open to learning about the other.

After describing the nature of analog and digital codes in chapters 1 and 2, I then note, in chapters 3 and 4, the great importance of the right and left brain hemispheres to analog and digital differences. Chapter 5 introduces the cultural crisis of today as analog hunger in a digital world. Chapters 6 and 7 identify the problem as extreme uncontrolled digitalism, with a focus on transhumanism. Chapter 8 presents ways to recover analog life, and chapter 9 makes clear that we need both codes. Chapter 10 provides a solution that seeks to integrate the two codes in the service of the analog from a distinctly religious perspective.

But before we can get to the personal and social crises and a proposed resolution, we must first understand analog and digital codes. This may seem difficult, but it is rather easy and rewarding. You probably already know much about analog and digital, and in any case you will have some new and useful concepts.

Chapter 1
ANALOG AND DIGITAL:
HOW THESE TERMS ARE USED HERE

Human beings have only two basic ways of representing information, knowledge, understanding, and meaning: One is with analog codes, the other with digital codes. Evidence for this claim, the two codes themselves, and their impact on our lives and culture are the focus of this book. In particular, the two codes will be shown in the coming pages to have very different mental and psychological effects and very different social and cultural effects as well.

However, first we need to know what analog and digital codes are; then we will move on to their great significance. To begin: A code is anything that we can perceive and that stands for or refers to some other thing than itself. An *analog code* is one that has some physical similarity or *analogy* to its referent. The degree of similarity can vary (more on this later) but some similarity must exist. A common visual analog code of a person is a photograph of him or her. By looking at the photograph you can recognize its referent, assuming it is a reasonably good photo. Even a bad photo usually gives you some knowledge about its subject.

However, the most elementary, most basic analog code of anything is our direct sensory/perceptual experience of it. Your nervous system constructs a representation of what you are looking at or listening to or even touching. This sensory or perceptual experience is technically a kind of neural representation, or code, of whatever is being directly experienced. These analog codes are assumed to be so close to reality itself that we say, for example, when looking at a person: "I see you." I don't say, "My visual system has provided an accurate visual representation of you." Likewise, we say, "I hear you," and not, "I have an accurate acoustic representation of your voice." Although the codes are in our nervous system, they underlie our conscious experience, and this experience is understood as an experience of what is real. These sights and sounds and other direct sensory and perceptual representations are our most elementary and most *immediately meaning-laden* experiences. (More on this later.) That our nervous system creates a representation or code is made especially clear when we suffer from brain or neural damage. Apparently, under brain damage, as Oliver Sacks made clear, a man might mistake his wife for a hat.

Analog codes are often visual or auditory but also involve the other senses. The similarity of analog codes to the physical world means that an important property of analog codes is that they are continuous and connected throughout space for visual or tactile analogs, or through time for auditory analogs. This occurs because any analog experience is just part of the large surrounding context of sensory-perceptual reality.

A *digital code*, in contrast, is discrete and has *no* similarity to its referent. Indeed, digital codes are arbitrary. For example, in the United States most people have a Social Security number that refers to them. This number has no physical similarity to the person to whom it refers, and it gives no clue to your height, weight, sex, race, or even if you are alive or dead. Likewise, our credit card numbers, driver's license number, and the like, give no information about who we are. Furthermore, most digital codes are part of a system that has rules for how the symbols are to be put in a correct sequence, such as the grammar and syntax rules of a language, rules of logic or mathematics, rules for a computer program, or arbitrary rules for the way in which an organization or bureaucracy writes its orders, pays its bills, and so forth.

This difference between analog and digital codes is hardly new, since the two types in question are familiar in computer theory, and philosophers and psychologists have long made somewhat similar distinctions. Often philosophers refer to the different types of code as sign (analog) and symbol (digital).[7]

However, the distinction between analog and digital codes means they are *qualitatively different*, that is, these two codes are for us humans *incommensurate.* They are independent of each other and refer to different aspects of their referent.

It is true that an analog code can be transmitted in the form of a digital code, for instance, a photograph of a person can easily be put in a digital form. But an analog code in such a digital form cannot be communicated to a human when so coded. That is, although it is common for analog codes to be put into a digital code, nevertheless, they *cannot be understood by us* when in a digital form. A photograph in a digital code is a sequence of digits and in that form can be transmitted to a new location. Television and screen to screen transmission is a familiar example of this. But, as long as the photograph, say of your grandmother, is in a digital sequence, you cannot tell even that the digital code represents a photograph, let alone the photograph's subject. A digital string loses the important information about the spatial closeness of the different coded points, that is, which digits are above, below, or even near each other. In addition, people are not able to translate the digits (numbers) back into shades of black, gray, and white (much less into different colors) by normal inspection. No, *for a digitally coded analog to be understood by a human it must be reconstituted in spatial form* in at least two dimensions, that is, the image must be put back into an analog spatial form before you can recognize your grandmother. Likewise, digital recordings of music, now common, must be put back into analog sound waves so that the human ear and auditory brain can appreciate them.

The opposite failure, namely the inability of analog codes to convey digital information to a human is also true. For example, take a digital message, such as a mathematical proof or a legal argument written in English. A person cannot understand the proof or legal argument by looking at the image or picture of it, or by hearing it spoken, that is, by just looking at the physical properties of the message, the shapes of the letters and words on the page on which it is written or by listening to the sounds the person makes while speaking it. For example, the picture of a mathematical proof or equation (Figure 1-1), which is the analog representation of a proof, completely fails to convey its meaning to those looking at it unless they know its digital code.

$$C = 2\pi r$$

or

$$\nabla \times \mathbf{E} = -\frac{\partial \mathbf{B}}{\partial t}$$

Figure 1-1: Examples of a digital mathematical code

The person receiving the message must first know the language in which the message is written (English) or spoken, and much of the information in

7

languages is digital. You must know the meaning of the symbols used in mathematics (C=circumference; r=radius; what π is) and also the rules for sequencing symbols, and often even more of the digital code world on which the message is based for example on antecedent mathematical proofs, or the finer points of legal precedent and argumentation. The second equation is Maxwell's 3rd and the analog properties it refers to are known by only a few.

In addition, analog codes have no true representation of a concept such as zero, of either/or, or of true negation (in contrast to simple rejection). The familar analog X means "no" to some action but it does not mean zero.[8] Indeed, a symbol for zero as a number was a major digital invention that occurred in India long ago.

Even the above-mentioned Social Security Number cannot be understood by someone who does not know what the digits stand for. We have to learn numbers before we can do arithmetic. We are all familiar with the failure to know a digital code with special digital symbols and rules for sequencing them: foreign languages, many topics in mathematics, computer programs, and many other sorts of codes often let us experience our digital ignorance. As a very simple example, when I first saw them, I didn't know what the digital highway signs HOV or Hazmats referred to.

The important point is that the two kinds of code each provide *unique* information or knowledge that the other cannot. This principle is caught, to some degree, in the familiar claim that "a picture is worth a thousand words." In comparison, one can say that "a picture of a thousand words is almost worthless," because you must know the meaning of each word, and a picture of a word, by itself, has no apparent meaning.

Of course, not all words are completely digital, since most words, when actually spoken, have some analog properties such as the speaker's tone, or some sound symbolism or often strong associations with images. Good literature or poetry, for example, is in large part responded to or understood by the reader only after the poem's words have elicited various associated images or sounds—in short, analog associations. Often a large composite image or internal panorama is fully present in the reader's mind only at the end of a long passage or even at the end of several pages. Supporting this is the pychological evidence that when a person sets out to learn a list of words, those lists whose words are accompanied by associated images are much easier to learn than similar lists of words without associated images.

A list of words like "zebra, butterfly, smile, cloud" is much easier to learn than a low image list of words such as "common, sometimes, average, verify." Words with associated images are thus both analog and digital.[9] Some words have an analog meaning based on where they are articulated. The word "us" is produced closer in the mouth than the word "them"; the same for "I' as opposed to "you." Thus, keep in mind that purely digital words are not common, especially when spoken.

The analog-digital distinction is in an important way summarized by Wilden as follows:

> The analog is pregnant with meaning whereas the digital domain of signification is, relatively speaking, somewhat barren. It is almost impossible to translate the rich semantics of the analog into any digital form for communication.... This is true both of the most trivial sensations (biting your tongue, for example) and the most enviable situations (being in love). It is impossible to describe precisely such events except by recourse to unnameable common experience (a continuum). But this imprecision carries with it a fundamental and probably essential ambiguity: a clenched fist may communicate excitement, fear, anger, impending assault, frustration, "Good morning," or revolutionary zeal. The digital, on the other hand, because it is concerned with boundaries and because it depends upon arbitrary combination, has all the syntax to be precise and may be entirely unambiguous. Thus, what the analog gains in semantics [meaning] it loses in syntactics, and what the digital gains in syntactics it loses in semantics....[10]

Although the analog is filled with meaning, this also means it is given to false meanings, in particular to superstition and the kind of meaning found in most dreams.

Further differences between the two codes and their associated systems

The physical differences between analog and digital codes can be enlarged upon. Digital code symbols are discrete—like numbers, or letters of the alphabet, or ones and zeros in computer machine language—while analog codes are commonly continuous, often with a rather arbitrary boundary, such as photographs or drawings. In a movie, although the edge of the screen serves as a boundary, this usually is an implicit, temporary, and arbitrary limit that is left behind by the next image, especially if there is a change of scene. In addition, the viewers of a movie are often unaware of any boundary as they focus on the center of the image, thus leaving the boundary ambiguous.

Analog codes when auditory are continuous in time and complex, like most spoken language, while auditory digital codes are sequential, simple in shape, and discrete in character, as found in Morse code with its sequences of dots and dashes.

Digital code symbols are part of a *system* within which they function. Digital systems have rules that determine whether a given sequence is valid. As already noted, languages all have some kind of grammar or syntax governing correct usage. Likewise, mathematics and logic have rules for acceptable sequences. Organizations, such as corporations, have rules for how customer orders and office payrolls are to be processed; journals have certain styles and formats that must be used by their authors, and of course computer languages have very specific system requirements. If a violation of the rules occurs, the system often comes to a complete halt or, if processing continues, an error usually takes place. In addition, digital systems press for as few symbols as possible. That is, digital systems push toward homogeneity, toward sameness. As an example, in math almost always in an equation the goal is to show that one side is equal to the other side. The ultimate goal in mathematics is to reduce A as equal to A. In a sense the very ultimate goal is to reduce the many to the one.

The systems within which analog symbols operate are natural, clear, and less precise. Visual analog experiences must maintain continuity with each other so that the spatial connectivity is maintained. The surrounding context is what commonly allows an analog code to be interpreted. Sounds such as music and the human voice have typical analog code properties, hence they must also maintain continuity, or much of their meaning is lost. As mentioned, in spoken language much of the meaning is in the tone of voice and associated images or sound symbolism—that is, analog—plus, of course, the digital information contained in the words themselves.[11]

Types of errors made by analog and digital codes

In general, digital errors are uncommon, sudden, discrete, and sometimes very large, that is, digital disasters. In contrast, analog errors are frequent, gradual, on a continuum, and usually small.

Someone's tax return, after being run through a complex digital system, might print out the final digits as 001,000,000.00. One million dollars, instead of 000,000,100.00, one hundred dollars. An engineer at a nuclear power plant might pull the wrong switch and cause a meltdown, or a shopper might accidently press a cell phone button and suddenly phone the "really" wrong person. A dramatic recent example involved Facebook. A small computing error at their headquarters caused the entire system to go down for more than twenty-four hours and affected some 2 billion people. These digital errors are rare, sudden, discrete, and sometimes have large consequences. They can sometimes cascade into unpredictable large systematic failures.[12]

Another kind of a digital problem is that shown by what has recently happened with tractors and some trucks.[13] After years of their being made more complex in digital ways, it has become very hard to understand how to repair these vehicles when they break down. You can't look at a broken digital system and know the code needed to fix it. As a result, older tractors and trucks produced before vehicles were made digitally complex are now being valued. If they break down, many still know how the relatively analog engine works and how to repair it.

In contrast, consider the analog errors set up in barter. Every chicken is a little different in tenderness and weight; every basket of wheat is a little different in freshness and weight. Likewise, every silver dollar is slightly different in weight, especially after much use. These errors are frequent, gradual, on a continuum, and usually small.

Now, turning to the general nature of analog experience, we again find a big difference from the digital experience. Visual-spatial experience requires heterogeneity; in fact, *it requires the presence of differences, often contradictions, in order for vision even to occur.* The basic "logic" of such parallel and oppositional systems is roughly, "the more differences, the more contradictions, the better." It is change that our sensory, analog systems are designed to detect. Right now, the black print on white background that you are reading is an example. Black and white are differences, contraries or opposites, and this is what makes the print easy to read. Experiments with homogeneous visual fields and with images fixed on the retina make the same point, namely that an image, such as a triangle, that is fixed so that it always stimulates exactly the same retinal receptors causes the receptors to adapt, and after a short time, without any differences or changes, the stimulus simply disappears.[14] This requires a clever experimental procedure that cancels out all ordinary eye movements and also the normally ubiquitous small uncontrollable random eye movements. In normal vision, even a stimulus on which we fixate is from moment to moment stimulating a slightly different set of retinal receptors. This maintains the perceptual presence of the stimulus and with it our awareness of it.

Chapter 2
THE ANALOG TO DIGITAL CONTINUUM &
THE ANALOG TO DIGITAL PROGRESSION

Now that we know the basics about these two codes, we can move on to some more of their characteristics. The previous discussion emphasized, for the purposes of clarity, a categorical distinction between analog and digital codes or symbols. However, it will be useful to consider the idea that analog codes, in fact, lie on a continuum. That is, some analog codes are more analog and others less so.

In the present discussion we will concentrate on visual phenomena. As mentioned, the immediate visual experience of a person (that is, seeing the other person physically present in front of you) is a very good, probably the best, analog visual representation of that person. A less analog code would be a color photograph of the person.

Still quite analog, but less so, would be a black-and-white photograph of the person. Continuing further might be a black-and-white sketch of the person, taken from the last photograph. This drawing would certainly be recognizable as a person, and if well done possibly recognizable as that particular person, at least to those familiar with the person in question. The next step might be a cartoon or caricature as in Figure 2-1a. A still more reduced description of the person would be a simplified sort of stick figure, Figure 2-1b. This very simple representation still contains the analog properties necessary to identify it as depicting a human person, but no more than that. In fact, such a drawing is similar to pictograms representing a man, in many primitive written codes, such as cave drawings. Further abstraction of the pictogram might arrive at a symbol so simplified that there is so little analog information, as in Figure 2-1c, that few would recognize it as a symbol of a man or human and most would treat it as a digital symbol. The Chinese pictogram for human or person, however, is very close to Fig. 2-1c, especially if the figure is made with ink on a brush.

Of course, still further simplification could turn it into a totally digital symbol for everyone (Figure 2-1d). These figures represent an example of the analog continuum, with a discrete jump to the digital near the end of the continuum. Exactly where on the continuum this jump will occur depends on whether the viewer still recognizes the minimal analog properties of the code in question.

Figure 2-1: Hypothetical changes in an analog symbol for man. Figures 2-1a–1c are partly analog but in a decreasing amount of analog coding. (Compiled by author)

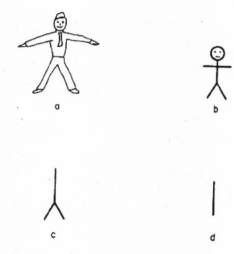

In principle, all sensory, perceptual, and symbolic experience can be put on the analog-digital continuum. Thus, this continuum is relevant to an enormous amount of human experience.

Also, keep in mind that emotional responses are part of analog meaning, and recall that analog symbols are commonly closely linked to meaning, which certainly includes emotions of all kinds.

Other Examples of the Analog Continuum

The familiar digital symbols of the first nine numbers and the earlier pictorial or analog character of the same symbols. Note the European "seven" shown to the right still has seven lines to it.

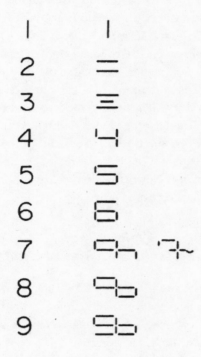

Figure 2-2: The first nine digits (numerals) as written today and when first used millenia in the past.

In the past, these symbols (Figure 2-2) were formed by straight lines, created by a stick marking in mud, and the code for each digit used the same number of lines as the number it symbolized, and thus was more analog; however today, thanks to changes brought on by brushes, pens, and now computers there is no longer any pictorial connection between the shape of the digit and the number it symbolizes. Another common example are the letters of the alphabet, which today have no visual similarity to the sounds for which they stand.

The Analog to Digital Progression

Now that we understand that analog, though not digital, codes can be more or less analog, we can explore the implications of this. A major claim of this book is that throughout history both the actual experience and the representation of human experience have reliably moved from analog to digital. This proposed change is termed the "analog to digital progression" and was implicit in all of the examples of the analog continuum just shown. However, additional examples will be given to make this concept clear. Furthermore, this analog to digital progression is assumed to have accelerated greatly in the last two hundred years, especially in the last few decades. Credit cards, computers, and the internet have been the major digitizers. The digital experience is one of abstraction and of confident certainty, but less meaningful than analog experience.

Walter Ong:
The Printing Press and the Rise of Digital Literacy

A major historical way, and a mostly positive one, in which society went from a primarily analog existence to a much more digital life is the movement of Western society from a primarily oral culture to one now dominated by written text. This change from oral culture has been documented by Walter Ong in an especially informative way. Ong never used the terms "analog" or "digital," but his understanding fits these concepts quite well.[15] He has shown how the printing press moved human understanding of the word from something oral, that is, sounded or spoken, to something visual, silent, and much more abstract.

The spoken word, as already briefly noted, has three kinds of potential analog meaning or association: 1. *Sound symbolism*, as in "thunder" or even slightly as in "smooth" and "jagged." 2. *Associated imagery*, as in words like "zebra," "butterfly" and "quietly," as compared to words like "often," "frequently," "associate." 3. *Emotional intonation*, which expresses the speaker's presence, emotion, and intention. Only emotional intonation is usually lost in print. In short, print and silent reading moved our experience from interpersonal, analog orality to a non-interpersonal, basically silent, visual digitalism.

As we will see, Ong notes that sounded words express power and action, and orality is redundant (repetitive) or copious. Orality is also conservative or traditionalist, and orality is close to the life world; it is agonistically (emotionally) toned, and is situational and involves others, rather than abstract, with a silent reader who is isolated from others.[16]

He summarized the concreteness of sound as follows: "Sound itself is related to present actuality rather than to past or future. It must emanate from a source here and now discernibly active, with the result that involvement with sound is involvement with the present, with here-and-now existence and activity."[17] As a consequence:

> An oral culture tends to be communal, non-individualistic, and authoritarian.... An oral culture stores information in memory and thus maximizes the word of others as an avenue to truth, stressing the reliance of mind on mind, of person on person. By contrast, a typographic culture, because it is strongly visualist, isolates the individual from the tribe even in much of its verbal activity, mutes and minimizes interpersonal communication, and elaborates the visual in all its aspects, including "observation" and "objectivity," as the preferred route to truth.[18]

Ong identified the printed word as silent, precise, visual, and abstract. By contrast, oral utterance "encourages a sense of continuity with life, a sense of participation, because it is itself participatory. Writing and print, despite their intrinsic value, have obscured the nature of the word and of thought itself. For they have sequestered the essentially participatory word—fruitfully enough, beyond a doubt—from its natural habitat, sound, and assimilated it to a mark on a surface, where a real word [that is, oral or spoken] cannot exist at all."[19]

To support his interpretation, Ong listed human sensory experience from concrete to abstract. The senses go in order of increasing abstraction: Touch—Taste—Smell—Hearing—Sight. Movement from left to right is "greater distance from the object physically; toward greater abstraction; ... toward objectivity, non-subjectivity"; "toward idealism, divorced from actual existence."[20]

He goes on to describe movement in the opposite direction, right to left, as a movement toward closeness "of sense organ to source of stimulus; toward concreteness; toward potency, indistinctness (sight and hearing are not easily confused with one another; smell and taste, taste and touch are ...)." In comparison, as noted, movement from right to left is also toward reality; "real as this stone I clutch."[21]

Nonetheless, Ong does give proper credit to the strengths of written language:

> Writing has made possible the vast evolution of consciousness that marks the later stages of human history. Without writing, not only tightly plotted lengthy narrative but also the kind of mental processes which go with the composition of even an encyclopedia article, not to mention more massive scholarly and scientific treatises, would be unthinkable in the fullest sense of this term. Oral culture cannot organize information in this sequentiality. Writing has made possible not only development of science and technology as well as the humanities (that is, the study of language, history, philosophy, theology, and other subjects having to do with man not as a physical being or an organism, but with man as a self-conscious being and thus with the life of the mind and with freedom); it has also made possible the complex relationships between large groups of people which a fully populated planet demands.[22]

In presenting this comparison of the spoken and the written word, Ong draws out for us the implications of the slow but truly major shift from oral culture to written culture, which is an example, writ large on human history, of the progression from analog to digital codes. He is also aware of how the printed word has affected our culture. "Yet it would appear that the technological inventions of writing, print and electronic verbalization, in their historical effects, are connected with and have helped bring about a certain kind of alienation within the human life world."[23]

He explains this as due to a cleavage created by print, a cleavage separating the knower from the external universe and subsequently from himself. This new separation makes possible a detached abstract analysis of humans and the cosmos but at the cost of splitting the original unity of consciousness and thus alienating man from himself and his original life world.[24] Again, we see what is described here as the difference between concrete analog and abstract digital experiences. Yet Ong is not unmindful of the great positive effects of print; after all, his own career as a professor and writer of books, including his books describing the lost positives of orality, are all expressions of the new, more digital, print technology.

Work and the Economy

The following examples of the analog to digital progression are given to make clear that the movement toward the digital is not just the result of today's highly developed technology but has a widespread cultural presence.[25]

Only a few hundred years ago, you could tell by looking at people's clothing and visible body movements what kind of work they were doing. Farmers and cooks and sailors and nursing mothers, priests and princesses all had different clothing and behaved differently. This is still true to some extent. But today most "workers" spend considerable time looking at a screen and wearing non-distinctive clothing. A person looking at a screen is doing primarily digital work that can be understood only if you know the codes being used. In short, work has become, for many, much less analog.

Still there exist largely analog jobs or occupations in which you can identify or understand by watching what the person is doing: a waitress, or a truck driver, house painters, and mothers doing child care. Jobs in which you actually touch the persons or the products you work with are typically analog.

As mentioned, a digital job is one you cannot understand by looking at the person working: for example, if a person is sitting in front of screen typing in letters and numbers, unless you are well versed in the language being used—French, Hindi, or Chinese, as well as such things as codes for different products, or variables, and so forth—you don't know whether the person is buying yen futures, solving a mathematical model of climate change, or ordering a replacement of noodles for some grocery. Most of these are the jobs of what Victor Davis Hanson calls the "credentialed class."[26] In short, the fact that work and the economies of the world have become more digital is obvious.

Time

In the past, time was understood in terms of seasons (summer, winter), months (the passage of the moon through its phases), and a description of the time of day based on the location of the sun in the sky or on events that occurred at regular times during the day. Years might be marked by major unusual events, such as floods, famines, or wars, or by who was the king or leader at the time. All very analog.

Thomas Merton well described the difference between the experience of time in the Middle Ages and his experience even seventy years ago, when he was writing:

> We who live in an age that has developed so many accurate in-struments for measuring out all man's activities into exact peri-ods of time and calculating the precise money value of every piece of work done and measuring the calories we consume and the vitamins we need, would find it hard to live by the easy and natural approximations of the Middle Ages. In a Cistercian abbey [and the nearby village] in the twelfth century the absence of the clocks and machinery and instruments and devices to which we have become conditioned gave the life of the monks [and villagers] a completely different tempo from ours. Their days had their own vital rhythm....[27]

This rhythm "followed the sun, the moon, the stars. It was integrated not into some abstract and mathematical norm of time but into the earth's ac-tual journey around the sun."[28]

During and soon after the Middle Ages, time got to be measured by clocks, then came watches. Time became a number like "two of the clock" then two o'clock AM or PM. At least morning and afternoon were distinguished, and most clocks had "faces" and "hands." This geometrical interpretation of the clock's face can be done analogically in the right hemisphere without losing one's train of verbal thought. Now, of course, with 24-hour time, an hour, a day, a month have become a string of digits. For example, early afternoon, on the fourth of June of last year is: 13,04,06,2023. Thus, time is now just digits in a string; when the digits change suddenly or start blinking and show a continually changing time they give a sense of nervousness, but not of time as the slowly moving hands of a clock do. Instead, cyberspace is without seasons, the virtual world has no day or night, and internet time has no relation to the sun's position.

Food

Originally our food looked much like the animal or plant we were eating. Meat especially has become more digital. Once, the whole animal might be cooked on a spit and then cut up into sections or different cuts; now, often even the bones are removed. Today the result might be chicken nuggets that have no likeness to a chicken. Hamburger has no clear analog connection to a cow or turkey or whatever animal it came from. Even greens now often come reduced to small pieces and in a package. On menus many items are listed with their calorie value.

Even more digital is the new push for artificial meat. No longer will meat represent an animal, raised at some farm and containing bones and a name like pork or beef, all giving it a genuine analog meaning. Instead, meat is planned to be some kind of digital mix of non-animal ingredients that might taste like meat.

Consider our present shopping experience of food and foodstuffs as compared to that of the past. In the not-so-distant past, to buy food people visited a variety of shops. They would visit the bakery where they smelled the wonderful aromas of freshly baked bread and saw and smelled other goodies like pies, cakes, and cookies. They went to butcher shops where they saw animals being cut up and prepared for us to eat. They stopped at green grocers where they saw piles of potatoes, other vegetables, and fruits. People knew directly about the wide variety of things that grow from the earth and how they looked, smelled, and how they felt to the touch. They went to cheese stores filled with pungent smells. At each store they talked with the sales people over the quality, possible use, and prices. Shopping for and later preparing food were strong analog experiences.

What is the situation today? Most grocery shopping is done in supermarkets. Here meat is sold in small pieces, often boneless, packaged in plastic. Cheese is so wrapped up there is nothing to smell. Vegetables are often wrapped in plastic and may even be pre-sliced. Packaged, prepared dinners make real cooking unnecessary. To cook you just push a few numbers on the microwave.

Now people can order groceries online; you see a picture of the kind of thing you would get but you don't actually see or touch and pick the *actual* item you buy. Your order comes to your door in bags and boxes. This kind of shopping is digital in the following ways: you no longer smell or touch most of the foods that you buy; you no longer talk with shopkeepers and salespeople. The food comes pre-packaged in ways that greatly reduce the analog character of the original. The most reliable aspect of your items is a number, the price.

Money

Recall that before money existed people engaged in barter, a very analog activity: my chicken for your basket of wheat. (Some people still barter, since it avoids the digital records that allow taxation.) After barter came the first metal coins, that is, money, typically made of gold, silver or copper. Such coins with intrinsic value were used for thousands of years, but eventually letters of credit between wealthy people or banks began to be used. Later, paper money backed by a bank, and usually backed by an analog anchor of value such as gold or silver, became common. In the last century in the United States, the analog anchor or backing of gold and then silver was removed, and now our money is just printed, not backed by anything of value. Money is created out of thin air by governments and sent to the banks.[29] Eventually it works its way down to the average citizen. Today in the United States, money has become almost totally digital. Even coins and paper currency are disappearing. Governments and businesses want to get rid of cash, the last small evidence of the analog. Economic behavior, which began in a strictly analog manner, clearly shows the progression of analog to digital codes over the millennia.

Our Names

Originally, even our first names had important associated analog meanings and were not just arbitrary sounds. Just a few examples: Abigail is "father's joy," from Hebrew. Andrew, from the Greek, meant "manly or masculine." Brendan originally was Welsh for "prince." Francis is the English form of the Late Latin meaning "Frenchman," ultimately from the Germanic tribe of the Franks, who were named for a type of spear they used. The original meaning of most first names had many different sources but typically now it has been lost; these days lots of new first names are being invented.[30]

English last names originally had analog meaning often based on occupation: Butler, Cooper, Dyer, Fisher, Miller, Tailor (or Taylor), Smith and so forth. Some last names initially came from a father's name: Johnson, Jackson, Jones (Welsh for "son of John"), and Anderson. Still other last names were based on physical characteristics—Armstrong, Long, Short—or where a person was from—Berlin, Churchill, Ford, Hilton (hill town), London.

Last names were usually given to an ancestor long ago, based on an analog characteristic at that time. Today these last name meanings, like first name meanings, are, in English, mostly forgotten or ignored. No one today expects someone named Baker to actually be a baker!

The big change in the analog meaning of names, however, typically comes when a name moves from its original language or culture to another. For example, German names like Bauer (farmer) or Hochberg (high mountain) or Crankheit (sickness) become in America just arbitrary sounds and strings of letters, totally digital.

Words, in General

As a rule, words began with some kind of sound symbolism or clear associated image value and then slowly became more digital, especially when the word went into a new culture or language.[31] Some typical examples: *ache*; is related to old high German exclamation for pain, "ah"; *barbarian* is traced back to those unable to speak Greek, who were mockingly accused of saying "bar, bar"; *maintain* comes from old French and Latin to hold in your hand; *paper* comes from a rush, called papyrus, from which paper was made; *sarcasm* has its origin in Greek meaning to tweak the flesh or make a cutting remark; *thirst* goes back to an Indo-European word meaning dry; *whisper* and *whistle* both descend from a Germanic word indicating a hissing sound; *yawn* is, of course, rather like it sounds.

Letters of the Alphabet

The letters of the alphabet were originally pictograms, that is, analog pictures of a related object.[32] The first letters represented consonants, and vowels were added later, especially by the Greeks. The letter A was originally, in the ancient Middle East, the image of the head of a cow (ox) with its two horns pointing up; it had a body with legs and often a short tail—a stick cow—and in the beginning it had two dots in the head representing eyes. The image stood for a glottal sound, something cow-like. It then became just the head of the ox, with the horns pointing up, no eyes; and the Greeks, not understanding its origin, turned it upside down, and we have today's capital A.[33]

Names and Images (Logos) of Organizations

Traditional image laden analog names of companies long were common, both for large, familiar names, like Ford Motor Company or International Business Machines, and for small ones, like Hudson Valley Gas & Electric. The name itself told you about their product or founder. But the names began to change. British Petroleum changed to BP; Sun Oil Company to Sunoco; American Telephone and Telegraph to AT&T; Tennessee Natural Gas Company to Tenneco; Minnesota Mining and Manufacturing, St. Paul, MN, to 3M (not knowing its past, at first sight one might think perhaps 3M is a bank?). The U. S. Rubber Company became Uniroyal. The Hong Kong Shanghai Bank, as it became global, changed to HSBC. The TD Bank was, first, just Bank of Toronto, then Toronto-Dominion Bank, and finally, dropping the associated images of Toronto and Canada, it became TD Bank, a "better," more abstract name now that the bank was doing business outside of Canada. Over and over, the specific and concrete name, with its clear associated analog image or meaning, is omitted, and the sequence of letters is then completely digital.[34]

Travel

The most analog, that is the most sensation- and perception- and body-based travel, is walking to some place; next would be travel by horseback, then by carriage, then by auto, and finally by jet airplane where the window view provides only limited analog experience. What systematically gets lost is the varied experiences of the more primitive, analog travel.

Sex

Sexuality is a naturally analog experience normally filled with meaning, but it is beginning to be less so. The recent popularity of sexuality can be interpreted as a widespread search for analog meaning in our digital world. Along with enjoyment of food and drink, sex has, at least, a kind of short-time positive emotional and therefore concrete meaning.

Nevertheless, today sex has less and less to do with real, that is, *actual* analog bodies, especially for men, and more to do with unreal images that are photoshopped. Men addicted to pornography are not addicted to real sex with a real woman. And now with sex robots, preprogrammed with words and movement, this new kind of sex has become almost digital sex.

Chapter 3
ANALOG AND DIGITAL CODES
AND THE TWO BRAIN HEMISPHERES

We now turn to how analog and digital codes relate to the two brain hemispheres; a topic probably anticipated by some readers. Neurophysiologists have long known that both analog and digital responses occur in our brain and nervous system, but there has been controversy over exactly how to identify the two neural codes in many instances. Apparently, this has been resolved by recent research. The difference between the two codes, as noted earlier, sets up a necessary difference in the location in the human nervous system where they are processed.[35] The reader very likely already knows that these two code types are in a rough sense located in the right (analog) and left (digital) brain hemispheres respectively. Apparently, neurons that respond to spatial and continuous information need to be separated from neurons responding to discrete, sequential information. Presumably this is also why analog and digital computing are kept separate from each other and not mixed together.

In general, for right-handed people the preceding distinction means, as noted, the right cerebral cortex is analog and left cortex is digital. Left-handed people tend to be the reverse but not as reliably as their right-handed friends and relatives. (The right-handed model is used here.)

There are two important points to make about using the terms "analog" and "digital" instead of right and left hemisphere:

(1) The results of analog and digital processing are available to a person's normal observation of external events and require no knowledge of underlying neurological activity.
(2) The distinction between analog and digital codes does not require any assumptions about where in the brain the underlying activity takes place, only that the two codes are processed in different brain locations.

Nevertheless, the hemisphere distinction is, in general, valid, and recent scholarship has made a very strong case for the social and historical importance of the two hemispheres in a way very compatible with the analog and digital distinction. The close connection between analog and digital and right- and left-brain hemisphere will, I think, become obvious. (In the past I made this explicit in three papers in 1983, 1988, 1990.)[36]

The most significant, and recent, example of this kind is a thoroughly documented, interesting—indeed profound—work by the neuroscientist Iain McGilchrist.[37] Because his brain science is solid, I will often use his interpretations of brain hemisphere differences as important support for my interpretations of analog and digital codes. That is, the present analog and digital model is parallel to McGilchrist's and is more easily applied to external and recent cultural phenomena but lacks the neurological evidence and important related interpretations of his approach, including his detailed interpretations of intellectual change in the West.

First, the two brain hemispheres have many differences that are physically observable. They differ in weight and size as a whole; they differ in the size and shape of several brain areas; they differ in the number of neurons and dendritic branching within areas; the ratio of white to gray matter is higher in the right hemisphere; the two hemispheres differ in sensitivity to hormones and to other significant biochemical responses.[38]

Second, and even more important, a great deal of research in physiology and psychology has established that the two halves of the brain cortex typically specialize in quite different psychological processes.[39] The left hemisphere is generally the intellectual and the verbal hemisphere, and because of the human emphasis on language, this hemisphere is often called the "dominant" hemisphere. This terminology is misleading, for in fact the right hemisphere is the major and more important hemisphere, as McGilchrist documents throughout his book.

The left hemisphere deals with much spoken and written language, abstraction, analysis, sequential logic, and related tasks. The core of left-hemisphere mental life seems to involve the manipulation of discrete symbols, especially sequences of such symbols. The left hemisphere codes and understands reality in strings of clearly defined events occurring in time, with language being the major expression of this capacity. Especially in adults, word recognition is lateralized in the left and face recognition in the right hemispheres respectively.[40]

The right hemisphere specializes in a very different type of mental operation. It is this hemisphere that responds to spatial information. It recognizes faces, patterns, and images of all kinds. And, importantly, it notices any changes in our perceptions. It is also the hemisphere that responds to sensory reality in terms of continuous wholes rather than separate parts; thus, it is the hemisphere of synthesis rather than analysis. The right hemisphere is the locus of our imagistic dreams. The right hemisphere is the hemisphere of most deep and complex emotion and of intuitive judgments about people and events, of our identity and the deep body-based understanding of the self.[41]

However, much anger seems to be a left hemisphere specialty. The left hemisphere is also specialized for specific motor response, for action, for grasping things. In contrast, there is evidence that such activities as music, sports, dance, and so on, which involve continuous, almost subconscious response to auditory, visual, spatial, and kinesthetic information, are concentrated in the right hemisphere, especially during the early learning stages.

In a masterful summary, McGilchrist writes, "the right hemisphere is particularly well equipped to deal with—our passions, our sense of humour, all metaphoric and symbolic understanding (and with it the metaphoric and symbolic nature of art), all religious sense, all imaginative and intuitive processes.... [These] are all denatured by the left hemisphere, which, by making them explicit, makes them, "therefore, mechanical, lifeless."[42]

McGilchrist goes on to mention other psychological characteristics: "The left hemisphere is competitive and its concern, its prime motivation, is power." The world it creates is "abstract and disembodied; relatively distanced from fellow-feeling; given to explicitness; utilitarian in ethic; over-confident of its own take on reality, and lacking insight into its problems...."[43]

Our auditory experience also has hemisphere differences. The right ear, more strongly connected to the left brain, is more sensitive to words or word-like sounds, while the left ear, more strongly connected to the right brain, responds more actively to environmental (non-verbal) sounds.[44]

An important way of understanding analog or right-brain processing is that it needs differences to function—in a sense the more differences the better. As already mentioned, the analog brain "likes" differences. In contrast, digital systems focused on abstraction reduce differences in the process of abstraction. As a result, digital or left-brain systems "dislike" differences, and the digital ideally reduces everything to the "one." An example is when a mathematical proof reduces one side of a mathematical expression to the other side, i.e., to A=A. The left brain apparently wants everything reduced to *one* and the right brain wants *many*.

Furthermore, analog codes are commonly saturated with both affective and immediately perceived meaning. Thus, most emotional experience, especially of sensory-based emotion, is centered in the right hemisphere. Also, sensory and perceptual experience is usually connected to every other such experience happening at the same time.

Right-hemisphere or analog experience has intrinsic meaning: there is no existential angst, no cool, skeptical rationality. In general people do not complain that a dream or drug experience was without meaning at the time of the experience, although it might not be a very rational meaning.

These days digital computers are the rule. But analog computing is still around. (The once popular slide-rule is an analog computer.) Analog computers typically use the magnitude of an electrial signal to represent a big number and and a small electrical signal, a small number. Also, analog computers don't use spatial images; instead they use codes that vary temporally or physically with the stimulus. The human sensory system appears to be primarily this kind of analog system. For example, a bright light or loud sound initiates a larger neural response than a soft light or soft sound.

The two brain hemispheres are connected by the corpus callosum, a wide, flat structure that allows information to transfer to the other hemisphere. However, McGilchrist provides a strong case that the corpus callosum primarily is used by each hemisphere to inhibit the other. This inhibitory function means a hemisphere has the ability to hold on to its autonomous functioning by suppressing the other.[45]

Some Qualifications

To the preceding general picture of hemispheric specialization must be added qualifications. Indeed—and this should not be too surprising—as the number of studies increases and as the questions asked get more varied, the specific evidence gets much more complex. McGilchrist is especially aware of how the two hemispheres work together, even though one may predominate, and he writes that each hemisphere plays some part in everything we experience.[46] Thus, for example, many tasks that were originally thought to be simple right- or left-brain tasks now are understood to involve various sub-activities, some of which take place in the other hemisphere. For example, reading is primarily a left-brain task but, of course, the pattern recognition involved in seeing and identifying letters has right-hemisphere components to it; the same is true for seeing and recognizing numbers. In short, it is no longer feasible to think in terms of an overly simple right-brain/left-brain dichotomy for many mental tasks. Nevertheless, there is good evidence to assume analog and digital codes are *primarily* processed in right and left hemispheres respectively.

It is also important to keep in mind that the analog-digital code difference, as already noted, clearly implies underlying neurological processing differences. Since these two types of codes are qualitatively different at the level of psychological experience, it is plausible to assume that their processing and storage should be differentiated neurologically as well. A simple difference would be one of location, and in the present case, as noted above, this would presumably be the right and left hemispheres, but in some instances the separation might involve different areas within the same hemisphere.

Nor would it be surprising, as already noted, if the neuronal functions underlying analog and digital symbols should be different. For example, the neurotransmitters that serve these two processes are known to be different.[47]

Two Kinds of Attention
but Not Two Kinds of Consciousness

A number of writers have proposed that the two hemispheres are each centers of a qualitatively distinct kind of consciousness. This idea is an oversimplification. Essentially, we have only one kind of consciousness, but what consciousness attends to can vary greatly. Our consciousness might focus on digital codes when writing a legal brief or a purchase order, but later focus on analog experience while playing tennis or practicing a dance. And many everyday activities, as noted above, involve both right- and left-hemisphere processes in an integrated type of conscious experience. Furthermore, we are quite aware during either kind of activity that our consciousness, with intellect (intelligence) and will (making decisions), are present in both types of attending.

Nevertheless, there is an important truth in the notion of two types of mental experience. Most of us are aware that our mental state is quite different when we are engaged in certain activities. For example, many sporting activities, such as golf, sailing, and mountain climbing, induce a mental state very different from normal experience, especially when the involvement is intense. There is a kind of total involvement in the sensory and perceptual world that results in the suspension of what can be called a verbally based "self-consciousness."[48] These strong right-hemisphere activities involve an intense absorption that can be most gratifying, not just because of the pleasure of the activity but also because verbal self-consciousness, with its anxieties about the future and self-presentation, has been suspended. For most people music seems to function this way, since musical perception for the great majority of people is primarily a right-hemisphere experience.[49]

There is also evidence, already noted, that emotional experience is somewhat lateralized, with the left hemisphere being associated with optimistic, superficial emotion and often anger, and the right with other, deeper emotions, especially when they are connected to people or are deeply negative.[50]

In short, there is often a clearly experienced distinction between the two brain mentalities as associated with immersion in either analog or digital codes. However, keep in mind that this difference in experience is the result of what our consciousness is attending to and focused on, and not a qualitatively different consciousness.

Gazzaniga and LeDoux articulated this position early in the brain hemisphere researches when they wrote that, in general, "the cerebral hemispheres in man do not oppose each other but instead work together to maintain the integrity of mental functioning."[51] Also, note that one of the important functions of the corpus callosum is to bring sensory and perceptual experience occurring on one side of the body to the other, verbal, digital side. The right hand very often needs to know what the left hand is doing.

Here is a quote from McGilchrist that clearly exemplifies how the two hemispheres *can* work together. We understand this as how analog and digital codes presumably do work together: "So the meaning of an utterance begins in the right hemisphere, is made explicit (literally folded out or unfolded) in the left, and then the whole utterance needs to be 'returned' to the right hemisphere, where it is reintegrated with all that is implicit—tone, irony, metaphor, humour, and so on, as well as a feel of the context in which the utterance is to be understood."[52] Indeed, there is good evidence that our body movements, that is, gestures, can contain information in them not found in the speech and that these gestures can then feed back into the process to alter thinking.[53]

There is, as already mentioned, evidence that our ordinary, integrated consciousness has a self-conscious quality derived from spoken language and probably based on, or at least controlled by, left-hemisphere processes. That is, language appears to be the integrating and dominant experience for much of human consciousness. Thus, right-hemisphere mental life is integrated into part of self-consciousness through language. The major right-hemisphere component of spoken language is, as mentioned above, what is known as "tone," the communication of the emotional state of the speaker, which goes along with the communicated information. This tone is extremely important, of course, for in some instances it can completely change or even reverse the information communicated. For example, "Yeah, yeah" can mean "no."

The expression "abstract or self-consciousness" is more appropriate to describe the mental life that is dominated by language and found in the left hemisphere, and "concrete or reality consciousness" might better describe the experience of pure right-hemisphere mental life, without the extra, language-based "self" component.

But, as noted above, our basic consciousness is the same for both hemispheres. This means that in both analog and digital processing, whether integrated or primarily in one hemisphere, we have a will and intelligence (reason). These two functions are needed for human consciousness. The two different ways that humans can respond to analog and digital codes are summarized in Table 1.

Typical Analog Experiences	Typical Digital Experiences
Continuous	Discrete
Spatial	Sequential
Image	Word
Holistic focus	Focus on parts
Synthetic	Analytic
Concrete	Abstract
Metaphoric meaning	Conceptual meaning
Spatial, as in performing: sport, dance, hunting	Sequential, as in writing: math proof, legal brief
Imaginative	Logic, rules
Parallel processing	Serial processing
Implicit/Intuitive	Explicit/Defined categories
Flow, change	Stasis, fixed
Reality	Virtual reality
Empirical observation	Theoretical prediction
Meaning: natural, strong	Meaning: arbitrary & weak
Deeply emotional	Superficially emotional
"Dislikes" no differences, "prefers many"	"Dislikes" differences, "prefers one"
Heterogeneity	Homogeneity

Table 1. Typical differences between analog
and digital code experiences for humans.

As shown in Table 1, these two activities, interpreting analog and digital codes, are psychologically—and physiologically—different. Also recall that the distinction between analog and digital symbols remains valid and clear, whatever the underlying brain location.

Two Kinds of Meaning

Analog meaning is always direct. Children, who rarely talk of meaninglessness, are constantly involved in direct meaning with the outside real world, and often with obvious real interpersonal experience.

Digital meaning is typically arbitrary. For example, the sound of a word *by iself* has no natural meaning once any associated imagery, sound symbolism, or voice tone is ignored. The sound "zebra" has no actual link to the animal. This is especially obvious when the code is a number or a systematic interpretation of a phenomenon like a stock market pattern or some other interpreted event. The digital is always an abstract experience never a concrete experience itself.

Chapter 4
FURTHER IMPORTANT PSYCHOLOGICAL DIFFERENCES BETWEEN ANALOG AND DIGITAL CODES

Here we take up the understanding of the brain hemispheres primarily as proposed by McGilchrist in order to understand still other important psychogical and social consequences of activity in the two hemispheres. McGilchrist describes the origin and difference of the two brain hemispheres as follows:

"Birds and animals—for they, too, all have divided brains—have to solve a conundrum every moment of their waking lives. In order to make use of the world, to manipulate it to their own ends, they need to pay narrowly focused attention to what they have already prioritized as of significance to them. A bird needs to be able, for example, to pick out a seed against the background of grit on which it lies, to pick up a particular twig to build a nest, and so on. But if that is the only attention it is paying, it will soon end up as someone else's lunch…, it needs at the same time to pay quite a different type of attention to the world—a broad, open, sustained vigilance, without any preconception of what it is that may be found, be it predator or mate, foe, or friend."[54]

To continue with McGilchrist,

"How to pay such contrary types of attention to the world at once?… The solution appears to have been the brain's separate hemispheres. Each of these neuronal masses is sufficient in itself and on its own to sustain consciousness…. Each can therefore attend to the world in a different way. What we call our consciousness moves back and forth between them seamlessly, drawing on each as required, and often very rapidly. For in humans, too, it turns out, the hemispheres pay different kinds of attention to the world."[55]

His insightful description continues, but I paraphrase. It is our left hemisphere, as in birds and animals, that pays the narrow, precisely focused, attention that enables us to get and grasp; it is our left hemisphere that controls the right hand with which we grasp something and controls the aspects of language that allow us to say we have "grasped" the meaning—made it certain and pinned it down. Meanwhile, our right hemisphere underwrites sustained attention and vigilance for whatever may be going on, without preconception. Its attention is not in the service of manipulation, but in the service of connection, exploration, and relation.[56]

Again, continuing with the McGilchrist distinction: a way of looking at the distinction would be to say that the left hemisphere's *raison d'être* is to narrow things down to a certainty, the right hemisphere's is to open them up into possibility.

"In fact, for practical purposes, narrowing things down to a certainty, so that we can grasp them, is more helpful. But it is also illusory, since certainty itself is an illusion—albeit, as I say, a useful one. There is no certainty. The more closely one pins down one measure (such as the position of a particle), the less precise another measurement pertaining to the same particle (such as its momentum) must become."[57]

By a rough analogy this implies that the more closely a bird comes to the location of a particular edible seed the more its attention moves away from other seeds and the less precise the location of other seeds become.

McGilchrist also notes that another way of characterizing the hemisphere difference is that the left hemisphere's world moves toward fixity and the right tends toward flow: "… the right hemisphere … sees things as a whole, never as isolated particles independent of a context." And "By seeing isolated points, the left hemisphere imagines that there are atomistically distinct entities, rather than seeing everything embedded in its context, which radically changes its nature; part of a web of interconnections."[58]

"This part-wise method of understanding, and resistance to the idea of things flowing and changing, together go some way to explain the left hemisphere's affinity for what is mechanical or inanimate."[59]

The right hemisphere is always interested in the differences which upsets the left hemisphere with its tendency to collapse unlike into like and see only what it is expecting to see.[60] The left hemisphere is *not* in touch with reality, but with its representation of reality, which is digital and turns out to be a remarkably self-enclosed, self-referring system of tokens.[61]

Turning to emotion McGilchrist notes "The left hemisphere is especially good at voluntary and social expressions of emotion, and one of the most clearly lateralized emotional registers is that of anger, which lateralizes to the left hemisphere. Deeper and more complex expressions of emotion and the reading of faces are best dealt with, however, by the right hemisphere."[62]

McGilchrist emphasizes that the left hemisphere understands truth as internal coherence of the system, not as any correspondence with reality as experienced.[63] In short, the "logic" of the analog and digital mentalities are quite different from each other, and often in direct opposition. In order to function a digital system requires carefully defined symbols, usually as few as possible in number. It requires clear, explicit rules for putting the symbols in sequences. A violation of the rules usually brings any digital process—that is, putting digital symbols into sequences—to a halt. There also seems to be pressure within digital systems to push toward the most general and powerful principles possible. That is, digital systems tend toward homogeneity, toward a reduction of the system to a minimum of rules and a minimum of symbols. The fewer the rules and symbols, the more rapidly and accurately the system can function (for example, in English the pressure toward simplified spelling is a typical digital pressure). Digital principles—such as precedent, rules for computer programming, the seeking of tautologies—all represent a pressure toward homogeneity, to equality, to a kind of conceptual egalitarianism, to A = A. Anything that makes one symbol equal to another symbol facilitates digital processing. By contrast, contradiction is much to

be avoided, since it brings the system to a halt, contradiction being a violation of the rules for sequential progression. These effects are summarized in
Table 2.

RIGHT HEMISPHERE	LEFT HEMISPHERE
Broad, holistic attention without preconceptions	Narrowly focused attention on a particularity
Direct experience of reality	Abstract representation of reality
Explores, seeks relations and aware of context	Concerned with getting a grasp on things to master them
Interested in the new from what it experiences	Focus on getting power from what it grasps
Not especially confident of what it knows or observes	Narrows to a confident certainty
Interprets experience as animate, living	Interprets experience as inanimate, mechanical
A source of deep, complex involuntary emotions	Good at voluntary, social expression of emotions, especially anger
Strong meaning, sometimes overwhelming or false	Meaning weak, arbitrary, or absent
Responds to context, often outside of any system	Rejects outside criticism, based on confidence in coherent, abstract system

Table 2. Right and left hemisphere mental and social characteristics.[64]

Some Social Consequences of Analog/Right Brain and Digital/Left Brain Differences

Recall that with digital activities there is an absence of intrinsic meaning.
The process, of course, has a kind of meaning—but those who know these
processes are well aware of the arbitrariness of the rules that allow the system
to work. There are different logics, there are many grammars, precedent is

always somewhat uncertain or accidental, and in much of science there are many different assumptions, all more or less equally meaningful, that could be used to build a model of a phenomenon. The particular symbols or elements used in the system are also often arbitrary.

Likewise, categories also are often arbitrary and unnatural with regard to who or what fits into them. The real world is a complex, continuous thing filled with context, and forcing our rich experience into simple, discrete categories often results in absurdities or in failing to address much of the relevant information.

An important consequence of the properties of digital systems is that those whose lives are immersed in them often suffer from a feeling of meaninglessness, from a sense of the absurdity and arbitrariness of life. As a result, when life is dominated by digital systems, only a few basic philosophic positions or attitudes appear possible. The most common response in such circumstances is to search for meaning in some ideology, such as communism or socialism, often combined with a low-level analog life of hedonism. These abstract intellectual attitudes or theories emphasize that diffences are either not important or are even evil—for instance, differences in class, which make aristocrats and capitalists the enemy. Typically the ideal future is a uniform world of the workers' paradise, where we all have equal income and there are no rich or poor. Ideology, as the name implies, is a predominately left-hemisphere system of knowledge.

More recently, globalism has ballooned and, with it, hostility to national and ethnic differences, along with a deep-seated primary concern with the universal capitalist measure of everything: money.

In contrast, the caste system of India is a mostly analog society. It has a great emphasis on observable difference, and this focus on visible differences and valorizing some differences at the expense of others makes it an extreme right-hemisphere society. Also, superstion is common in analog societies.

Fascism, with its emphasis on race, is also partly a form of analog extremism, and to that extent right-hemisphere-based. However, fascism has many ideological and digital characteristics. The very word "Nazi" is a short form of national socialism. But, nationalism with its focus on big government and government-based socialist programs is also heavily digital. Fascism, therefore, is a mix. In Germany it had a heavy emphasis on the Aryan race, thus a right-hemisphere mentality. But with its rejection of beauty and the fascist "uncompromising shredding of the past"and, above all, its great emphasis on the nation state, it was a very digital or left-hemisphere ideology.

Still another modernist digital position is that proposed by the positivists and linguistic philosophers, who explicitly denied not only all analog meaning but even metaphysical assumptions—in short, they rejected or viewed with extreme skepticism all knowledge or experience coded in nondigital forms.

Another solution to the absence of meaning is to accept digital codes as the only acceptable type of code, and to accept that digital systems are intrinsically absurd, but then to propose that the answer is to "create" meaning through personal, conscious choice, through decisions and commitments. This is an existential solution. (More about analog and digital implications for our present cultural situation later.)

A final digital world chosen by some is the world of scientism, that is, the belief that only matter and random based evolution exist. There is no purpose or overall meaning.

Whether individuals choose materialism, political ideology, or existentialism they have explanation but no real meaning. Beauty, love, goodness, and especially the transcendent worlds of spirituality and faith are excluded. And, to the extent that their views involve or get them involved in the world of banking and capitalism in general, the dollar becomes the measure of meaning. As was said by Oscar Wilde 150 years ago, such people are cynics who "know the [digital] price of everything and the [analog] value of nothing."[65]

The popularity of the preceding philosophies, most especially of ideologies in the twentieth century, can be interpreted as a response to the increase of digitalization and the general lack of meaning brought about by the growth of digital life. That is, these positions follow from the implicit assumption that digital codes are the only legitimate, or primary, codes for knowledge. The problem is that, at best, digital codes provide references to things and sometimes explanations of things, but not their meaning.

Turning to the right hemisphere and to analog mental life, we note a very different kind of worldview. Visual-spatial experience requires heterogeneity; in fact, it requires the presence of differences, often contradictions, in order for vision even to occur. As already noted, the basic "logic" of such parallel and oppositional systems is roughly, "the more differences, the more contradictions, the better." It is change, commonly involving cause and effect, that our sensory, analog systems are designed to detect.

Also as mentioned above, contrasting with digital political systems are analog systems, which are based on differences, especially certain differences that are given a special priority. As mentioned, ethnic politics are analog in character, as are those that emphasize heredity, race, tribe, or caste; and such politics are often bolstered by superstitous beliefs or by some kind of story, myth, or religious justification for their social heirarchy.

Left-Brain Autism and Extreme Masculine Thought

One way to understand and identify sex differences is to note extreme types of male and female characteristics. In any population there is a variation around the mean, and it is often helpful to look at the extremes. Here we look at the importance of hyper-male types of brain function. Simon Baron-Cohen has provided good evidence that men, on average, are more abstract, logical, systematic, and hierarchical in their thinking, and they are usually more interested in the physical world than in people and relationships.[66] This is an advantage for a scientist, mathematician, philosopher, theologian, or any kind of systematic thinker.

Baron-Cohen has recently described this kind of thinking as intrinsic to men—that is, natural to the male brain—and also as implicitly *autistic*.[67] He proposes that extremely autistic thinking is hyper-masculine, and autism is much more common in males than in females, by about a 4 to 1 ratio. The truly autistic person is one who is "mind-blind"—that is, low in empathy and incapable of understanding other people as having minds, in particular of having thoughts, feelings, and intentions.[68] Some autistic people seem to be unaware that others even have such mental properties. Instead, people are just objects or things, like the rest of the inanimate world.[69] Such a world is one that is cold, empty of any interest in others, and without any relationships or emotions. In terms of what matters to most people, such "objective" knowledge is without any human meaning and therefore lacks most of what is of real interest to them. (It is interesting that oxytocin apparently stimulates the social brain regions in autistic children.)[70] Of course, most scientists and abstract thinkers are not seriously autistic, but if it is a benefit in such disciplines to be able to reject emotion as bias, reject intention as inadequately knowable, and require logical connections, observable material facts, and systemic order, then being somewhat autistic probably helps. In other words, scientific disciplines such as physics and biology incorporate the underlying set of assumptions that also characterize autism. This understanding of science came in with Galileo, Francis Bacon, and Descartes, among others, and it has helped create the modern model of the lonely, empty, machine-like universe devoid of all but mechanistic meaning. By rejecting the relevance to science of a personal God and by rejecting any property such as purpose or intention, such men set up today's autistic digital nonhuman emphasis.

In conclusion, a very relevant interpretation of today's digital world-views is that extreme digitalism emphasizes abstraction and great certainty, and it is not, therefore, in touch with reality but with a self-referencing abstract system. The digital also emphasizes fixity rather than flow; the mechanical or inanimate and hyper-male, autistic set of starting assumptions. All of this involves an implicit, often pathological rejection of the body, intentions, emotions, and interpersonal relationships. It dominates our mental world at the price of life without meaning.

Chapter 5

ANALOG HUNGER IN A DIGITAL WORLD: THE CULTURAL CONFLICT TODAY

The concepts of analog and digital have major applications to our present culture, and we start with the underlying *concept* of brain hemispheres. McGilchrist outlines in detail how the development of our present culture has been a systematic process of growing left-hemisphere dominance, especially since the end of the Medieval period, and that today the modern West has become so left-hemisphere-dominated that this dominance is the source of our current cultural malaise. His thesis is

> that for us as human beings there are two fundamentally opposed realities, two different modes of experience, that each is of ultimate importance in bringing about the recognizably human world, and that their difference is rooted in the bihemispheric structure of the brain. It follows that the hemispheres need to co-operate, but I believe they are in fact involved in a sort of power struggle, and that this explains many aspects of contemporary Western culture.[71]

I assume that McGilchrist's work thoroughly justifies the general hemisphere distinction and its application to social conditions. However, from an analog and digital position we enlarge on this position of McGilchrist and other related critiques of modernity.[72]

General Loss of Personal Identity

A major contemporary phenomenon is the search for identity by large numbers of people. Identity means "who I am: what are my traits and abilities and weaknesses, what are my goals and what are my personal relationships, and to whom do I belong, who is my family, mother, father, what group or groups am I part of?"

As we will see, the lack of identity leads to many ways of expressing what is here called "analog hunger."

For example, in *Modernity and Self-Identity*, Anthony Giddens gives a description of the disruption of space and time

> required by globalization, itself the necessary consequence of industrial capitalism, which destroys the sense of belonging, and ultimately of individual identity. He refers to what he calls 'dis-embedding mechanisms,' the effect of which is to separate things from their context, and ourselves from the uniqueness of place, which he calls 'locale.' Real things and experiences are replaced by symbolic tokens; 'expert' systems replace local know-how....[73]

We turn to specific ways of losing our identity

Loss of Family Identity

In the past, people's identity was closely related to their family and their family traditions. With the large increase in dysfunctional families, this major source of identity has greatly weakened. In the old days if you were one of the Smiths from Elmtown, you and much of the town knew who you were: they knew your parents, grandparents, crazy uncle and weird aunt; they knew what your family did for a living and probably where you went to church and had gone to school. Now, with so many divorced, blended, and single-parent families, plus dysfunctional "normal" families, interpersonal-based family identity has greatly weakened.

Loss of Physical Location

The physical location of where we grew up and are from has faded significantly in recent decades. Today, if you grow up in the Louisiana Bayou country, you may have more of a link with people who grow up in Manhattan, because you shared the internet and with whom you played video or other games on your phone. Even the old distinctions of being a Southern (Rebel) or Northern (Yankee) have often disappeared. Indeed, being an American is no longer a reliable source of identity. Often, we are hyphenated Americans—African-Americans, Hispanic-Americans, Asian-Americans, and Euro-Americans. In addition, many people in the governing classes are globalists; they may have two or more passports, they often live part of the year in other countries and consider themselves not to have a definite national identity. Of course, the loss of place also tends to reduce loyalty to any place, including a reduction in patriotism.

Loss of Stable Work or Occupation

In the past many people used to have an identity because of the nature of their work. They were farmers, or machinists—or housewives or mothers. Or they came from a family of accountants or lawyers. Now even farmers and truck drivers spend much of their time looking at screens. In addition, people's actual jobs keep constantly changing. It is now common for people to reinvent their work lives and the company they work for—and with it their work-based identity—several times in the course of a lifetime. People no longer work only for General Motors or IBM or Exxon and no longer have a lifetime of a fixed job identity before they retire.

Loss of Religious Identity

Also, for many people, religious identity has faded. In the United States and in Europe the decline in religion is well documented and well known.

And finally, I believe because of all of the above factors there has been a serious loss of friendships among, especially, the younger generations.

In short, the conditions that "grounded" a person's identity in the past have often dissolved. In terms of our present discussion, these were all analog conditions—based in our body, our bodily activities at work or in the family, expressed in interpersonal relationships, and rooted in a particular place, context, or the practice of religion.

Trans-Speciesism as a Response to Identity Loss

Before getting later to the transgender issue, it is useful to look at those who find an identity in a new species. Recently you can seriously identify as being a dog, a cat, a parrot, an elf, or fairy, or even a dragon. For example, there is a man who calls himself "Spot," who enjoys dressing as a dog, and who walks around on a leash as a dog and is fed treats. There is Eric, who lives life underwater with a latex tail as a merman. A woman says she is a cat, born in the wrong species, and hisses at dogs. A half-naked, web-footed woman claims to be a mermaid. Another woman lived as a horse every day for seven years by trotting on all fours and eating grass. A transgender woman who began as a man, now, at age 55, has had her ears and nose removed to transform from a woman into a dragon with scales, a forked tongue and a horned skull, all involving extensive surgery. There is also the man who identifies with being a parrot who has cut off his ears, colored his eyes, and added many tattooed feathers.[74] As an extreme is the Frenchman who describes himself as a black alien. Note how in many instances the person has made physical changes to their body. There are school children claiming to be cats.[75] Also, a Scottish killer and transwoman prisoner claims she/he is an infant and demands baby food and diapers. Even trans-age claims are now showing up![76] Images of these trans species humans are available on line. Look them up and be amazed.

Apparently, there already are a large number of people who identify with animals, at least to some degree. One such group is known as the Other Kin Society.[77] This group includes those who identify with higher animals that exist or have existed and also dragons, which are presumed not to have existed, at least as commonly understood. There are also people who understand themselves to be elves, for example.[78] There are at least two other groups of people besides Otherkins who seriously identify as animals, one group called "Furries," and the other "Therians." (See internet for these groups.)

All persons in these groups identify, at least partially, as non-human. These communities include people who understand that they are a werewolf or other were-animal, mermaids, vampires, as well as the more common dog and cat people. Many of these new identities involve painful experiences, for instance, surgery, but pain is also an analog experience and

46

it gives meaning. The countless young people today who actively cut them-selves are also using pain as an analog experience that gives meaning.

These new identities are facilitated by internet contacts and, according to some, by the meaninglessness of much of modern life and by fears about the future. As a result, these people searching for an identity are showing examples of "analog hunger in a digital world." They are expressing clearly "It is about showing who you are."[79] After all, animal life, pleasure or pain, is thoroughly analog and more or less digital-free.

Another common way of finding identity these days is the enthusiasm shown for smaller political groups—Scottish nationalism being an example of the breakdown of the more abstract United Kingdom. The many forces in Europe now working against the European Union, and for its breakup, are examples of the return of national or ethnic identity.

A common expression of this search for a new identity is the emergence of secessionist sentiments in the United States, whether in the state of California or Texas, or in some of the counties of Oregon or Virginia. The de-sire to maintain or to establish a more concrete and local kind of identity is becoming clear.

Yet another example of recent "ethnic" identity is the development of gay identity. Contemporary gays have a flag and have parades, in much the same way that previous ethnic identities did, like the Irish or Italians. And, of course, what used to be our male or female sex is now up for grabs with different genders and various terminologies. In a modest way, the popularity of tattoos can be seen as a way of getting a visible analog identity.

The Crisis for the Young

The absence of strong analog experiences is especially damaging to the young. The older generation using the new digital media know who they are and welcome the convenience of digital media, but the young who begin their lives without a basic immersion in analog life are very vulner-able.[80]

As mentioned, the large increase in dysfunctional families, commonly without strong interpersonal bonding in the family from birth through adolescence, means many are growing up with a weak internal analog iden-tity based on active bodily and family experiences. This is furthered by the absence of bonding with young friends, which continues their weak interpersonal and emotional life.

This interpersonal weakness is often combined with little bodily experience with the outside world based on physical activities, in the playground, or with early chores, or with sports. Cell phones, video games, and the internet all drastically reduce contact with the varied external world. As a consequence, these children have a weak and limited sense of their body and its relationship to physical reality. These young individuals literally don't know who they are interpersonally. It is relevant that many transsexuals are autistic, which results in much interpersonal weakness.[81] Obviously immersion in virtual media contributes to a poor body-based identity. Young persons who spend more time with digital media than with experiences of physical reality don't know what their body can do, or how their body relates to the physical world. In short, they are without a body-based identity. I describe them as *analog-empty*. Often, they search for and create an identity wherever they can, usually on the internet with its digital "reality."

Transgenderism

Transgender young people can be seen as a clear case of a misplaced expression of analog hunger. Fed by virtual reality, and interpersonally in dysfunctional families, many children never thoroughly experience their own body as male or female or in relationships with others as a boy or girl.[82]

Analog to Digital Progression in Political Theory

We have already seen that digital left-hemisphere thinking is abstract and not about concrete reality; it focuses on the internal consistency of the abstract system. On the political left, the basic political concern *begins* in an analog way. The issue is usually helping the poor and disadvantaged, and then perhaps the lower levels of the working classes, since they are relatively poor and disadvantaged. These concerns are obviously good. And people of the political left usually identify with this kind of positive moral understanding. The problem is that these desirable analog concerns morph over time into a digital ideology, in which people are classified into a few types—normally the good workers and the bad capitalists, or today the "deplorables." This, of course, does great violence to the actual nature of many human beings and develops further into things as abstract as the Communist or Progressive ideology. As noted already, all ideologies are digital.

However, at least in the United States the same kind of development has occurred on the political right. The political right *begins* with freedom and with free enterprise, that is, the socially good analog desire of creating a needed product and, with it, jobs. But, as a company prospers and grows, it becomes larger and more complex, and it begins to focus less and less on the analog product and its workers and more and more on simply making money. They are not just making a good automobile, they are now speculating in metal futures, in foreign currencies, and the management discovers that these new activities make more money than selling cars. And, of course, various forms of tax evasion also become important from a strictly monetary point of view. Thus, what was once free enterprise has morphed into capitalism, where the only focus is on dollars, which are obviously digital. The associated rationale becomes a kind of capitalist ideology. Furthermore, the general culture in the capitalist society continues to focus increasingly on consumption and with it, of course, money, that is, digital dollars, and everything now has a digital price.

G. K. Chesterton saw this years ago:

> It cannot be too often repeated that what destroyed the Family in the modern world was Capitalism. No doubt it might have been Communism, if Communism had ever had a chance.... But, so far as we are concerned, what has broken up households and encouraged divorces, and treated the old domestic virtues with more and more open contempt, is the epoch and Power of Capitalism. It is Capitalism that has forced a moral feud and a commercial competition between the sexes; that has destroyed the influence of the parent in favour of the influence of the employer; that has driven men from their homes to look for jobs; that has forced them to live near their factories or their firms instead of near their families; and, above all, that has encouraged, for commercial reasons, a parade of publicity and garish

novelty, which is in its nature the death of all that was called dignity and modesty by our mothers and fathers.[83]

In an important sense, the last 250 years have been the two hands of communism and capitalism unknowingly co-operating. Both left and right have been moving the culture, primarily through growth of the government and technology, to increasingly abstract and digital systems. No wonder these two traditional opponents have often recently merged.[84]

Perhaps not so obvious is that *all* of our dominant economic systems are extremely digital. Let's take three traditional systems that are commonly thought of as conservative. For example, laissez-faire capitalism, popular with libertarians, assumes we are isolated autonomous persons and ignores our context of commitments to others and to society itself. Economic nationalism assumes the great centrality of the modern state with its inherent, large, dominating, digital systems. Finally, democratic capitalism, perhaps the name for what we have at present, is obviously based on digitalized money and huge government programs. The culture as a whole struggles to survive on fading analog organizations like family, religion, and once regionally based sport teams.

Still another example of digital capitalism in action is the industry of tourism. Here all cultural differences have dollar values and are turned into a pleasant entertainment for visitors. The differences don't really exist as important or genuine; instead, they create a pleasant consumer experience, like different cuisines, which keeps the economy of air travel, hotels, and tour buses going. Tourism is thus a money-making business that undermines whatever life remains in the analog society it takes you to visit.

A brilliant and well-known interpretation of this is the concept of "market totalitarianism," described by Robert Bellah, as similar to state totalitarianism.[85] It also might be called "money totalitarianism."

Meanwhile, capitalism through its relentless focus on the dollar price has digitalized life even for countless so-called conservatives. They become more worried about their money than about their culture, or religion, or conservative values.

Along with this relatively quiet digitalism of the right, the most visible politics is on the left with the progressive movement's concern with differences, such as racial or sexual. But this is only a concern to make differences unimportant or equal—as already noted, a regular digital emphasis.

Finally, recall that the left hemisphere is both very competitive and very concerned with asserting its power because of its over-confidence in its interpretations. These are obviously both very capitalist and very communist values. As a consequence, this new left-brain world is abstract and removed from fellow-feeling.[86]

Chapter 6
DIGITAL IMPERIALISM

High-tech companies, such as Amazon, Apple, and Google are producing a digital product that then is used to both provide and, in the process, control more and more human services. A curious change about those who run these companies is that the great majority of them are now progressives, people of the left. In the past, such business leaders tended to be conservative, people of the right.

Recent examples include Uber and Lyft, both relatively new companies, both providing a large-scale digital service and both coming out politically as progressive by opposing pro-life policies in Texas and advocating for abortions.[87]

As already noted, digital workers, left-hemisphere types, routinely assume that as persons, they are superior to the deplorable blue-collar analog workers because of their education and skill. Besides being called the "credentialed class" they are also described as the "managerial elite" by Samuel Francis. I call them the "digital class." Earlier these groups or classes were proposed as the high IQ and average or low IQ classes by Murray.[88] Other theorists just called them the new elite class.

Most billionaires appear to be digital types. (Of course, this is not so true of those who inherit their billions.) For example, George Soros made his first multimillions by betting that the British pound would drop,[89] all done through electronic codes used to speculate on currencies. Currency trading, along with almost all financial speculation, is now done in completely digital systems.

More and more of the very rich are becoming liberal. In the past the rich were usually conservative or at least Republican. But then the old businesses were analog since they made or sold real things like railroads, or oil or soap or they made automobiles. The new very rich are all in digital systems and so they have become liberal or progressive like all left-hemisphere-focused activities. Analog business leads to conservative positions and digital business results in liberal positions. Thus, we can account for the recent change that the liberal democrats are morphing into the party of the rich elites.[90]

By the term "imperialism" I mean extending power and dominion by gaining economic, internet, and often political, control of others. Imperialism is used because of the psychological tendency of digital explanations to create such certainty that criticism is met with arrogance and anger. This attitude comes with the implicit or explicit assumption that the critic is ignorant or stupid. Such a rigid attitude is common in our country's present digital class.

Second and more important is the enormous economic power this class has and the still greater wealth that they seem certain to have in the future. Right now, digital systems are creating billionaires but are destroying thousands of small businesses. New digital technologies, especially those based on block-chains, are beginning to remove countless white-collar banking jobs. Driverless trucks have already begun to be used and could in a few years make millions of truck drivers unemployed. Even many service jobs, thought of as intrinsically requiring a person, are being digitalized, now especially in Japan. In all these cases relatively simple analog work is being replaced by a digital system, often based on AI.

A still-existing example of this is the difference between the economies of the American eastern and western coasts compared to middle American and southern states. Joel Kotkin describes this schism as "between two ways of making a living, one based in the incorporeal world of media and digital transactions, the other in the tangible world of making, growing and using real things."[91] He describes the two digital coasts as trying to repeal geography, that is, analog reality.

In addition, the huge, recent growth in income disparity is almost entirely due to digital billionaires and the others who support them. They herald a new feudal, class-based society: An upper digital class on the top, perhaps 20 percent of the American population, plus the large hardly employable analog class of "deplorables" beneath them.[92] (An insightful sociological and historical treatment of such a prediction is provided by Dominic Green.[93])

The understanding of technology as a powerful danger to all humans has long intellectual history, but here this danger is put in a wider, more detailed context that involves the two brain hemispheres and the visible process of digitalization. A good example of the earlier understanding is "…modern technology has become something else and more than the main formative influence of a new civilization—mankind faces technology as it once faced nature itself, that is, as an overwhelming power against which protection must be sought."[94]

Over the prior thousands of years most humans developed and survived on analog skills. Humans, long focused on hunting, gathering, farming, cooking, child rearing, and similar analog activities that are now suddenly facing a powerful digitalism.

Negative Effects of Digital Media

Cell phones

Some of these new effects are serious forms of psychological and social pathology or what has been called a "mass sociogenic illness." Behavioral or emotional problems were found in 6.3 percent of a large sample of children and adolescents and in 16 percent of an adolescent sample.[95] Most disturbing is the clear evidence for frequent addiction or semi-addiction to iPhone use resulting in a sudden and a widespread increase in anxiety and depression. Researchers found that smartphone use was, in fact, associated with symptoms of anxiety and depression, as well as increased experience of stress. The more participants used their smartphones, the more likely they were to experience symptoms associated with these disorders and report being stressed. (See studies cited below.)

To begin, here are some statistics. Almost 95 percent of Americans own cell phones and 77 percent own smartphones. Around the world, smartphones were used by 1.85 billion people in 2014, which was expected to be 2.32 billion in 2017 and 2.87 billion in 2020. Obviously there are even more billions using cell phones today.

A major question is how do we get to know we are addicted to our cell phone? Here is evidence for addiction or obsessive cell phone use: When a person uses his or her cell phone most of the time, is unable to cut back on cell phone usage, uses cell phones as a solution to boredom, and feels anxiety or depression when the phone is out of range.[96] Adolescents seem to be at high risk of being smartphone addicts.[97]

First, a relevant question is: Why would you expect negative psychological effects from excessive cell phone use? The answer is that cell phone use involves long time periods of primarily digital attention and involvement. Cell phone behavior is mostly the focused pushing of small keys with numbers or letters on them with little time out for direct analog experience. There is some restricted analog experience of virtual images, but the dominant experience is a rather intense digital one. It may be hard to remember, but virtual is not actual. Also, when on a cell phone a person has cut themselves off from all the surrounding real analog world.

We will look at a representative sample of research on cell phone usage. Jones found that many seemed to be addicted to their mobile phones and it was concluded that the excessive smartphone use had a negative psychological effect.[98] Another study[99] was conducted on mobile phone usage by students from Central Switzerland. It was found that mobile phone usage during night hours was common among youngsters, and they reported poor perceived health based on such usage.

An investigation of psychological health effects and digital stress with 1,557 German internet users also found negative psychological effects.[100] Researchers investigated whether anxiety and depression independently contributed to smartphone addiction using a large random sample of Lebanese undergraduates.[101] They reported that depression and anxiety were positive predictors of smartphone addiction. They found, also, that depression scores were a more powerful predictor as compared to anxiety.

Another study[102] reported that an intensive increase of cell phone usage among teenagers in the year 2012 was associated with the symptoms of depression, suicide risk factors, and suicide rate.

Cell phone addiction was negatively correlated with academic performance in many studies.[103] Another experiment used a random sample of 100 college students and, although some students enjoyed their cell phones, they found that many other users had negative psychological effects and suffered from depression and anxiety.[104] Thomée et al., 2011, in a systematic study of young students aged 20–24 with a one-year follow up, concluded that high cell phone usage was associated with sleep deprivation and symptoms of depression for both men and women.[105] De-Sola Gutiérrez et al., 2016,[106] report similar effects. Other researchers examined the predictive factors of smartphone addiction in middle school students in South Korea.[107] They reported that teenagers who spend more hours on their gadgets are more at risk for suicide. Another study by Augner and Hacker[108] reported that low emotional stability, chronic stress, and depression have a positive correlation with amount of phone usage.

In short, from these and many other studies, it is confirmed that adolescents' negative mental and sometimes physical health is associated with cell phone addiction. Research strongly implies that excessive cell phone use causes anxiety, depression, and sometimes suicide.[109]

Negative Effects of Digital TikTok

Another cause of serious mental suffering arose from TikTok, a social media platform, where users create and share videos. During the COVID-19 pandemic, the use of this site greatly expanded. References to tics and Tourette syndrome content also increased dramatically at the same time, as did the number of patients with tics seen in neurology clinics. One study compared the phenomenology of "TikTok tics" to typical tic disorders. The researchers chose to analyze the most widely viewed videos and therefore focused on the most popular content creators. Videos with the keywords "tic," "Tourette," or "tourettes" were reviewed to identify content created between March 11, 2020, and March 30, 2021. They performed a quantitative assessment of TikTok tics as well as a descriptive analysis of the entire series of the relevant videos. Results showed that the mean age of the cohort was 18.8 years old, and the majority were women. Unlike the predominance of facial movements in typical tics, they report arm movements were most frequent. The average tics per minute was 29, and almost all recorded TikTok tics were severe, causing significant disruption of behavior. Whereas coprolalia, that is, frequent, involuntary use of obscene language, and self-injurious behavior are infrequently encountered in typical tic disorders, they were present in the overwhelming majority of TikTok creators. Conclusions: TikTok tics are distinct from what is typically seen in patients with Tourette syndrome, but they share many characteristics with functional tics. Although the exact nature and causes of these tics vary and remain to be worked out, these tics can be considered, in part, as an example of mass sociogenic illness. The tics involve behaviors and associated emotions spreading spontaneously through a group.[110] There even are reports of addiction and suicide linked to TikTok.[111]

Virtual Reality: Illusion, With Its Basic Negative Effects

The single greatest harm of the new digital media is the way that virtual reality has become the actual reality for so many, especially the young. When virtual images and sound are used as aides to our normal, natural, already existing analog contact with people and the environment, there is no problem. But once we use virtual reality to create a virtual self, for example, to "meet" new people, we have created an illusion that we treat as real. In this new fantasy world, the two actors can be whatever they want to be. The basic digital effects are that the person you are communicating with presents only a virtual image, that is, a digital reality, that is almost perfect, objectively not themselves, and thus unreal. In virtual reality almost all people present an image of themselves carefully constructed and smiling. Likewise, the images of their house and yard are always especially positive. This kind of communication creates envy and anxiety in those who see the other as perfect or almost so. The anxiety is a consequence of treating the unreal digital virtual image as true, as actually normal, and real. A person's virtual reality is a kind of fantasy that, if it were created just in the mind, without virtual technology, would be seen as psychotic.

Another major source of anxiety set up by virtual communication is that your messages are given a number, the number of people who gave you a "LIKE" response. This digital "LIKE number" becomes a measure of your goodness, or success. You now remember not the actual positive experiences of an event but the number of likes it got. Then you begin to feel anxious as the number was lower than the last such event or is lower than the number sent out by friends. Experience is converted from a right-hemisphere analog memory of actual experiences to a number of likes competing with your past and especially with others.

No wonder people claim to be dragons, cats, and members of the opposite sex when one's own identity is subject to so much digital anxiety.

The Decline of Science to Reduce Digital Imperialism

Finally, a decline of science as the highest level of truth is needed, since science has been the major source of extreme technological growth. The ideology of scientism with its materialistic and reductionist assumptions has been an important element in digital imperialism. Thomas Molnar made clear the then-dominance of science as a worldview when in 1988 he wrote, "The truth is, one cannot harness technology without demoting science as a master-concept."[112]

Obviously, science is at the core of the analog to digital progression and the dominance of the scientific worldview; therefore, it needs to be and is being challenged. Not science, in principle, but science as a master-concept, as the only source of accepted truth. In the 1980s when Molnar was writing he thought that such a challenge to science was inconceivable. Decades later this seems much more probable.

First, Science Has Developed a Major Problem with Replication

All kinds of studies, especially in biomedicine—for example, cancer research—and also in social science, have failed to be replicated when actually tested again. Unfortunately, journals and authors are both anxious to publish something that claims an effect that has been found. Too many of the published effects seem to be due to chance, and the motivations of those involved do not appear to include verifying claimed effects. Actual fraud appears to be rather common. Even research money to replicate existing supposed findings is hard to get, and failures to replicate are not welcome at most journals.

Second, the anti- Western postmodern movement with its anti-reason and anti-science interpretations has further eroded the prestige of science

This "progressive" position sees science as a Western white man's hegemony that should be rejected to support women, other races, and cultures. Their postmodern understanding is an intellectual current characterized by the more-or-less explicit rejection of the rationalist tradition of the Enlightenment but the acceptance of theoretical discourses disconnected from any empirical test, and by a cognitive and cultural relativism that regards science as nothing more than a "narration," a "myth," or one social construction among many others.

Postmodernism is also a force against the important analog or right-hemisphere characteristics at the center of Western culture. A brilliant counter critique has been provided by George Steiner in his book *Real Presences*.[113]

Unconsciously, social science supports the postmodern position by developing a science of man that forbids itself from speaking reasonably about the nature of man. Instead, social science has contributed to the "destabilization" of man with its postmodern assumption that there is no human nature, only constantly varying social constructions. Implicit in this underlying assumption is the postmodern critique of rationality and even science. It means history, social science, even most psychology can now be interpreted however you like. Postmodernism has landed in the abstracted left hemisphere and fled from fact.[114] (That this is now becoming true of basic natural science is noted below.)

Third, science, has become something of a "hired gun"

In conflicts of many kinds each position, for example, left vs right now cites its own science. Science has become so complex and expensive that it is now very dependent on money and support, especially from the government or other large systems. The old saying is still quite true: "Those who take the King's shilling soon wear the King's uniform." Science now seems to support controversial government policy or to be captured by corporate interests or even by political correctness. At its beginning modern science was a generally independent activity, but much science has become a gigolo for the government or for other groups who pay for it. It not uncommon for negative findings to be denied or unreported. Witness the scientific conflicts over the nature of COVID-19 and the policies to respond to it. This lack of independence has undermined much of science's intellectual validity.[115]

ANALOG HUNGER IN A DIGITAL WORLD

Fourth, the problem of relevant untested variables

Especially in biological and psychological research this issue is serious. Physics, in contrast, is pretty good at reducing an experiment to one of very few possible untested variables, and most of those that might affect the results are usually known. Biology and psychology run studies, however, where many possible other causes could be operating but are not tested for and are usually unknown. For example, assume a good study shows that a particular vaccine reduces deaths and the spread of the disease. Then because of the "science" this vaccine is required for a large population. Years later, however, new research shows that the vaccine greatly increased the probability of another illness, or reduces fertility, increases still births and genetic defects in young women or, perhaps, reduces the sperm count and increases abnormal sperm in young men. Finding simple effects and ignoring all the other possible outcomes and then demanding compliance can be very dangerous and is a way of using science as a kind of fascism.

This same issue plagues psychological research, as well, where a finding could be caused by any of a number of characteristics of those investigated—characteristics that were not tested or measured.

Fifth, science is increasingly seen as a source of frightful destructive power and thus as something to fear

The fear comes from the cannons and poison gas of World War I, the atomic bombs of World War II, the anxiety about nuclear conflict between nations, and recently the deep concern about biological war in which a nation might use virus-based plagues on its enemies. Biological science began its human impact by saving us from various diseases, but today it is being used by some countries to create new diseases.

Sixth, and finally, many scientists have begun arguing for abstract principles that are incapable of being tested

Historically every scientific theory had to be testable to count as science. But experimental evidence, long the standard for whether a proposed hypothesis is true, is, by some, being phased out. For example, the claim that there are an infinite number of universes makes our very particular world something to be statistically expected. This multiverse position is acknowledged as impossible to test. In such a claim, scientists have cut the link between analog observation of empirical reality and digital abstraction. "The digital puts an end to the *age of truth* and introduces the *post factual information society* ... which elevates itself above fact based truth."[116] (Italics in the original.) However, we know that such digital interpretations are arbitrary and soon cease to be meaningful as new digital interpretations get proposed.

As a consequence of these six points, I suggest that downgrading our estimation of science to a more moderate level is a harbinger of a coming more sensible new era.

Chapter 7

TRANSHUMANISM:

THE ULTIMATE DIGITAL IMPERIALISM

The "trans" movement, in all its forms, is fundamentally digital. As already noted transgenderism consistently attempts to blur the differences between male and female, to make them unclear and even unimportant. However, the focus of this chapter is on transhumanism.

I have noted various disturbing digital developments. But what is the most disturbing is that many transhumanists today explicitly seek the end of human beings as we know them. This position, using a digital-based AI (Artificial Intelligence), is often clearly articulated by transhumanists. Transhumanism is now a large movement, with its own conventions, and even a journal. We will look at its general goals and the clear positions advocated by major transhuman theorists such as Ray Kurzweil,[117] a prominent advocate of transhumanism.

The transhumanism movement is pushing for a new form of life that leaves human beings behind, as a less developed life-form. Some of the transhumanists expect humans to become the "household pets" of the new digital-based species. Many such theorists just think that human beings will become irrelevant—if they are not actually wiped out by the new AI creatures.

At present, if anyone were to advocate turning a certain group of humans—some race, some religion, even an entire nation—into slaves or pets, much less advocate their annihilation, such proposals would rightly be attacked and vilified. But those who call for such treatment of all human beings are considered advocates of progressive modernism. But in fact, these advocates should be labeled as expressing "hate speech."

Certain transhumanist theorists such as Ray Kurzweil predict what he called a "singularity," namely a specific time, in the near future, when machines will become smarter than humans. The transhuman future will then become inevitable in the near future, as less intelligent traditional humans fall behind their AI competitors.[118]

Some transhuman theorists advocate a few positive goals, such as using sophisticated AI to help people avoid pain. Some want to help humans to live much longer, perhaps forever. Thus, the goal is sometimes to create a superior human being. But if people could live forever, I am not sure they would be human in the present sense of the word.

Transhumanist ideas are presented as exciting, positive, and inevitable because of today's very rapid development of computer power, medical technology, and robots. In short, transhumanism claims that science and technology will soon allow the creation of "a new being freed from all biological constraints."[119]

To free us from our biological nature, to escape from our bodies, is, of course, to "free" us from analog life. The human body is dismissed by these theorists as of no importance to being human. Instead, the "human" will be expressed in some non-biological medium of AI and computer programs—but not one that is like any biological form. Just as a computer program can exist in different physical mediums (e.g., magnetic tape, electronic pulses in a silicon-based computer), the new human will be found in a new physical medium. The natural body is understood as an impediment to the development of the mind. The soul has, of course, disappeared from this kind of thinking.

Transhumanists also claim that human beings, when freed from biology, would no longer have any unique rights or status. Other entities, with similar levels of knowledge and "personhood," whether they are new animals, cyborgs, machine intelligences, or aliens, would be of equal moral significance to human beings.

These post-human beings may treat existing humans as pets. Here are some examples. Mathematician and founder of information theory, Claude Shannon, said, "I visualize a time when we will be to robots what dogs are to humans, and I'm rooting for the machines."[120] The co-founder of Apple, Steve Wozniak, claims, "robots taking over would be good for the human race" because they will be "smarter than us" and will make us "like the family pet and take care of us all the time."[121]

Even a partial transhuman development would make "old fashioned" analog humans a big problem for this new digital society. Traditional analog humans would become the poor, the large lower class of underlings. As such they would cost lots of welfare and be a realistic source of violent rebellion against their digital masters. These are good reasons, even prior to a complete take-over, for those in power, that is, the digital systems owners and AI programmers, to control traditional humans and even do what is possible to reduce their numbers.

Transhumanism and Gnosticism

The link between transhumanism and Gnosticism is also a key link to understanding transhumanism. (Gnosticism means ultimate meaning or redemption can be acquired through some kind of special knowledge.) The first known expression of the transhuman goals was around 100–200 BC in a movement later called Gnosticism. Modern transhumanism is a kind of neo-Gnosticism,[122] a connection recently noted by others.[123] Like the original Gnostics, transhumanists by rejecting the body reject also Judaism and Christianity. As a consequence, religion will now become an important part of our critique of digitalism.

Although Gnosticism was complex and varied, the core Gnostic beliefs expressed very clearly their commitment to abstract knowledge and their rejection of the human body. This rejection of the body brought with it, of course, a rejection of procreation and fertility, combined with a special Gnostic hostility to women. Women were understood, because of pregnancy, birth, and nursing, as especially "embodied," and as a consequence Gnostics were commonly anti-woman.

The first traces of Gnostic systems can be discerned some centuries before the Christian era.[124] They were explicitly hostile to Old Testament Judaism. Gnostics denied the understanding found in Genesis that humans were created by God, in the image of God, and that we were created male and female. Later Gnostics denied that the Christian goal was eternal life in heaven. These Gnostics wanted the extinction of human life itself. In a word, they were extremely hostile to the Judeo-Christian tradition.[125]

The Gnostics could do little about reaching their goal, as the technology then was very primitive; they could only withdraw from society, not have children, and advocate that others should join them. But today

64

transhumanists, because of sophisticated digital AI, now claim that the end of humans is possible, indeed in sight. (For a fuller view of Gnosticism in order to see how dominant it has become in our time, and how it is advancing in part through the digital world, see Kutz.[126])

A number of heterodox authors and movements that became strong in the first Christian centuries are generally termed Gnostic. These Gnostics claimed their knowledge was superior to Christian orthodoxy's knowledge about the content and path of man's "salvation." Though some Gnostics accepted certain parts of Christianity, they promoted a form of abstract spiritualism. Gnostics believed that "Dualistic distinctions between 'body' and 'mind,' 'soul,' and 'matter' are meaningless. All things are ultimately one. Each person has within him/her a spiritual seed which is consubstantial with the divine.... The illusion of multiplicity [meaning especially the individuality of human beings] vanishes once the person knows the true reality.... It is the knowledge that you and God are one. To know God is to be God."[127] Again, there is no "Many," only the "One," and this is of course very digital.

Perhaps the most significant aspect of Gnosticism as it relates to the life—individual and collective—of humanity today is its attack on human sexuality.

Ancient Gnosticism, in advancing its negative program concerning human sexuality, attempted to present its position as anti-materialistic, anti-hedonist, while acknowledging that some of its elect did slip into the seeming opposite notion of reaching "salvation" through immersion in aberrant sexual behavior. But the objective of aberrant sexuality was pleasure, without any chance of reproduction. Thus, God's plan for creation to populate the earth would be rejected.

A Gnostic scholar, Ioan P. Couliano (or Culianu), states that for the Gnostic theologian Marcion the greatest tragedy was not the creation of this world but the creation of mankind. We were, he states, "out of low-quality materials—that 'flesh stuffed with excrement' that makes humanity the slave of procreation...."[128]

Filoramo, another Gnostic scholar, cites a considerable number of Nag Hammadi tractates where there is open, misogynistic language that expresses "the same thought: *women as such cannot enter the kingdom of heaven.*"[129] "The *Gospel of Thomas* ends thus: 'Simon Peter said to them,

'Let Mary leave us, for women are not worthy of life.'" Gnostics claim that Jesus said, "Every woman who will make herself male will enter the kingdom of heaven."[130]

This goal that women should become like men seems to be the goal of many radical feminists. Women should become high achievers in business, science, technology, engineering, and mathematics, earn black belts in martial arts, get into the special military forces, and so on. Women are always being encouraged to become more like men, and no attention is given to genuine feminine strengths and virtues. Love, having children, empathy, nurturing interpersonal skills, and being mothers are ignored or rejected.

Gnosticism is thus a movement of radical opposition to God and His plan for humanity. It seeks by every possible means to end humanity. The dominant transhuman ideology of today contains important aspects of the original Gnosticism. First, it rejects the body and the body-based experience of reality that we have by contact with real people and things. It rejects our human nature, which comes through our sense perception and bodily experience.

How does all this relate to the digital world? Digital (AI) theorists propose that they will create a future reality that promises unlimited power and well-being to the new "human beings." Digitalism has already created an artificial and destructive world of sexual pleasure through pornography. There is a segment of highly educated people behind the transhumanist movement, which promises that present man can be redesigned through artificial intelligence to become "superman" and the controller of all reality, like a god. Transhumanists did not invent the digital world, nor did they create many of the technologies that have produced much good in the world, but they are pushing digital technology to extremes to change the nature of reality, and this requires developing more and more control that makes people totally dependent on the electronic world for access to goods, services, and information. Many people familiar with AI have noted its potential for grave harm to humanity.[131]

We also today see an effort to tie people—especially the young— more and more to the digital presentation of reality, that is, to virtual reality. We see an attempt to control, to disparage, and even to conceal what is genuine reality and its associated common sense. Omitted, or at least neglected, are such basic phenomena as frequent contact with living people, the enjoyment of normal activities together, work on actual things, abundant contact with nature, and the like. These experiences represent the basic analog world, where the meaning of things is easily discernable, where especially the reality and meaning of each human is known, where men and women meet often in the context of family gatherings and discover the importance of interpersonal relationships, marriage, and children.

Chapter 8
RECOVERING ANALOG LIFE
AND PERSONAL IDENTITY AND MEANING

Return to the Real

We need to mount a strong response to the pathologies created by unbalanced digitalism and its transhumanist goals. First, we must be observant and aware both of the growing digitalism in the world and of its effects on our own lives and on those people we love and care about. Second, we need to remember that the analog world is not just the world of our experience of reality; it also gives us the world of meaning. Thus, we must return to the world of reality. The digital world only gives us abstract explanations, not genuine meaning. For us humans, meaning in the world comes from our experiences of beauty, goodness, and truth.[132] We find meaning in nature, as when we see beautiful flowers, and in the smile or hug of a child as evidence of love. Meaning also arises directly out of making things that require our active participation, such as baking a pie, plowing a field, sewing a quilt, going fishing, or playing a game. These are analog experiences, and it is in such experiences that we find meaning.

Today many are already responding to this analog hunger, to the desire for the real. Two books by David Sax explicitly and forcefully advocate analog activities. His suggestions are generally valid and useful, though I am much more critical than he of today's extreme digitalism.[133] Another example of analog rediscovery is the "Craftmanship Movement." Robert Pirsig wrote in his book *Zen and the Art of Motorcycle Maintenance* that through engaging in craftmanship activities one creates a good life.[134] Richard Sennett in his book *Craftsmanship* also speaks of the importance of doing a job well and contends that work with our hands is crucial.

Sennett claims that work with our hands has been seriously neglected in today's capitalist economy.[135]

The importance of craftsmanship receives further expression in Matthew Crawford's *Shop Class as SoulCraft* (in the British edition the book is titled *The Case for Working with Your Hands or Why Office Work Is Bad for Us and Fixing Things Feels Good*). Crawford shows how our culture has devalued manual work, and he speaks of the increasing meaninglessness of office work.[136] He makes a good case for choosing a trade instead of attending college, if one wants a life of meaningful work. White-collar work has so often separated thinking from doing, and in the process has deprived most office work of meaning. White-collar work too often has become a kind of mostly passive, meaningless, digital activity—in contrast to analog and meaningful, active, manual labor. Peter Korn speaks of "a shared hunger" to make things.[137] Eric Gorges expresses a similar understanding in *A Craftsman's Legacy: Why Working with Our Hands Gives Us Meaning*.[138] These authors all make a powerful case for a major turn toward a more hands-on kind of work, and away from what is available in our digital economy.

A related but even larger movement is called "Back to the Land" or "Back to the Farm." This social phenomenon is significant in England and the United States, and it has advocates around the world. In *Six Steps Back to the Land*, Colin Tudge makes a strong case for an "agrarian renaissance."[139] In *A Small Farm Future* Chris Smaje explains how to build a small farm.[140] Many British organizations devoted to similar values and goals have endorsed these books. One well-known American advocate of the return to a more rural, local, and decentralized society is Wendell Berry, who supports the positions of the Southern Agrarians of an earlier era.[141] In the United States and Canada, a large, interconnected movement explores and promotes everything from small-scale green environmentalism to organic and small-scale farming.[142] Some people wish to return to subsistence farming, others focus on preserving special tracts of the environment. These movements tend to be very critical of both capitalism and big government. In any case, they all represent a desire for contact with natural reality. They advocate respect for and return to the analog world in all its concrete variety.

In still other ways, this search for the real is already happening in the movements toward smaller political units. The immediate answer to creeping digital imperialism is to return to the real, which at its best and strongest avoids digital technology completely.

Here are some additional places where we see analog hunger, and the need for analog experience. Not all who need the real know that they do! While contact with nature has positive emotional effects on the well-being of people[143] and there are definite cognitive benefits from interacting with nature,[144] there is also, unfortunately, good evidence that most people have become increasingly distant from nature. S. and P. Kesebir looked at popular English-language culture, including fiction, song lyrics, and film story lines, since 1950. They reported a marked decline in references to nature.[145]

Real Activities: Women's Analog Underground

There is now a large under-the-radar internet of activities expressing women's need for the real. Relevant websites and podcasts show women enjoying all kinds of special activities, some of them rediscovered and precipitated by the COVID crisis. These activities include baking, cooking, preserving, gardening, flower-growing, quilt-making, and sewing of many types, as well as all kinds of discussions of child rearing and positive family activities. Here the digital internet has well served analog needs. But these women don't just meet via virtual reality, they often meet in person and talk on the phone. They create real interpersonal relationships.

The Benedict Option

In his important book *The Benedict Option*,[146] Rod Dreher proposed an analog response to what I term digital secularism. His focus is on the growing anti-Christian character of today's progressive culture. He argues that Christians should opt out of the secular culture. Dreher is also aware of how we are controlled by our technology. He sees the need to opt out of the present consumer system, which supports a post- and anti-Christian society. The Benedict option involves a serious commitment to community, new schools, child rearing, food growing, and many other basic analog activities.

Real Communities vs. Networks

Almost all of us belong to communities and networks. What is the difference between a community and a network? The former is analog, the latter digital. Here are the differences in detail:[147]

1. Communities are small and intimate. Networks are large and anonymous. 2. Communities are organic, bottom-up. Networks are artificial, top-down. 3. Communities require action and contribution. Networks encourage passivity and consumption. 4. Communities are attached to a place. Networks can be location-independent. 5. Communities nurture the whole person. Networks divide a person into parts.

Real Education

We need a return to the real in education. Much education today is abstract and does not engage the body. Students do not learn to do any actual physical work, with sports and theater being exceptions for a limited number of students. The Montessori movement stands in strong contrast with this; it represents a way of keeping in touch with reality in the education process. The Montessori method emphasizes a hands-on approach to learning, where the child learns by working with materials and not just by being told. Montessori also includes learning projects outside the classroom in the natural environment, such as growing a small crop of vegetables or raising chickens or even pigs. In short, Montessori emphasizes right-hemisphere learning, while not rejecting left-hemisphere book learning.[148]

Radical Responses to Digital Imperialism

More extreme reactions exist; they will be mentioned briefly because their significance is obvious. Some are worrisome, but all are interesting.

One is "Get off the Grid." This would mean no computers, no cellphones, no internet. It represents an obvious response to an awareness of the dangers and harms of our present society. It is not possible for most of us, but it has a future.[149]

Another is "Break up digital monopolies." This means not only breaking up large systems but opposing the growth of the federal government; building local independence.

Yet another is the "secession" movement. The case for political secession, once thought very extreme, has been receiving much more support recently. There are counties in eastern Oregon that want to leave Oregon and join Idaho. Some political and social commentators have noted that different large parts of America don't agree with each other and might constitute as many as five different countries. Some think that a break into a red-state country and a blue-state country now makes sense.[150]

Luddite-style action is a possibility. The Luddites were English workers in the early nineteenth century (1811–1816), who destroyed machinery, especially in cotton and wool mills. They did this not because they were against all technology, but because the new industrial mills were destroying their jobs and way of life as cottage-based weavers, thus destroying their lives. They were obviously not successful, as the industrial revolution rolled over their opposition with the more efficient factory-based method of producing fabrics. What was a small problem in the beginning of the industrial revolution appears to have become a much larger one now as we approach the end of industrialism. Now we face a future where the number of potential lost jobs is huge and where few new jobs for humans are created. Contemporary Luddite action might involve destroying internet towers, blowing up data stored in buildings that constitute the Cloud, disabling corporate and government internet sites, an so on.

Yet another possibility is major violence against digital structures. By far the most explicit call for a revolutionary destruction of our technological (digital) system comes from Theodore Kaczynski who echoed the earlier quote from Churchill. He proposed violent destruction of our technological systems. From his off-the-grid cabin, this Harvard graduate and Ph.D. in math—the notorious Unabomber—has argued that the deepest human values and most respected human qualities are becoming meaningless and obsolete because of our techno-world. He wrote:

> What is the meaning of personal identity if you are someone else's clone? What is the meaning if your innate achievements have been planned for you by bio-technicians?... Without free will what is the meaning of freedom or moral choice?...

prevailing concepts of traditional values like loyalty, friendship, honesty, and morality have been seriously altered by modern conditions. Courage has been devalued. Personal honor has practically disappeared. In the future with intelligent machines, human manipulation of other humans' genetic endowment, and the fact of living in a wholly artificial environment, conditions of life will be so radically different, so far outside the range of anything that the human race has experienced in the past, that all traditional values will become irrelevant and will die. The human race will be transformed into something entirely different from what it has been in the past.[151]

Kaczynski presents a prediction about how this might actually take place, namely that such a technological future will develop in a rationally unplanned way and not at all wisely. The history of our existing technology is a good example of the unplanned, unpredicted, and unexpected. A catastrophe such as the "singularity"—the taking over of human beings by super-human AI—could also take place because of the natural, unplanned AI growth.[152]

Kaczynski argued extensively that our technological progress is bringing inevitable disaster and that only the collapse of our technological civilization can avert this disaster. He went on to the extreme conclusion that this requires the "necessity of revolution," one of physical violence.[153]

What, then, are we to do? McLuhan warned us years ago, "Once we have surrendered our senses and nervous systems to the private manipulation of those who would try to benefit from taking a lease on our eyes and ears and nerves, we don't really have any rights left."[154]

Chapter 9
THE ANSWER: NO EXTREMES! WE NEED BOTH ANALOG AND DIGITAL

Although at the present time serious resistance to encroaching digital imperialism is needed, we must avoid both extremes. Perhaps we forget that extreme analog is also often awful. Extreme analog means no writing or reading, hence no Scriptures, no novels; no numbers, hence no mathematics, no science. Each code compensates for a serious weakness in the other.

The Bronze Age Pervert (BAP) provides a disturbing, perhaps slightly horrifying, proposal to return to a purely analog society, as outlined in his *Bronze Age Mindset* and on Caribbean Rhythms podcasts.[155] What he proposes represents an intense reaction to the dominance of leftist political identity over many decades. Bronze Age Pervert calls for (1) the recognizing, rewarding, and institutionalizing of inequalities amongst men, and the true hierarchy of biological types; (2) the rejecting of individual rights; (3) the dominating of the weak by the strong; (4) the elevating of pirates, conquistadors, and warlords as the highest and freest type of men; (5) the preparing for struggle and war; (6) the promoting of command and obedience; and (7) the promoting of some form of military-monarchical rule, seen as the best form of government. The BAP thus supports violence, some forms of racism, and extreme forms of masculinity.

Furthermore, this movement explicitly rejects reason and mythologizes a pre-rational period, before the historical development of Greek philosophy. In short, BAP has a total right-hemisphere emphasis and thus represents a completely analog approach to identity and society. Such a rejection of the digital is not only impossible, it is also a rejection of the great positive digital benefits for all people. Reading, writing, arithmetic, countless machines, and yes, computers, upon one of which I am writing this book, have brought previously unimagined good things.

Tolerance

Given the existing intense conflict in American and much of Western culture between analog and digital groups, the first thing needed is for the two groups to learn to tolerate each other. Until that happens, no positive resolution is possible. We can start by recognizing that our culture gives us many shared truths that today we seem to have forgotten, especially those underlying our constitution and our republic.

The recent intense hostility between progressives and conservatives is unfortunate and even in some ways stupid. We can promote tolerance by recognizing that each position represents important truths.

Cooperation

We also need a principle for how to understand cooperation between analog and digital mentalities. I propose the following: the digital should be in the service of the analog. This means that the digital should, as a general rule, be subservient to the needs of the analog, and not to itself. The digital is to serve us in our bodies, not to replace our bodies and bring about our extinction. There is a profound case for this principle drawn from the brain-hemisphere perspective by McGilchrist in *The Master and His Emissary*. He says the "emissary" (left brain) needs to be serving the "master" (the right brain).

Let us look at some examples of the digital in the service of the analog. One of them is postal zip codes. These are familiar to us in the United States and have greatly increased the speed and efficiency of mail delivery. Bar codes are other example. These codes are now common, especially on grocery goods, and greatly facilitate payment and checking out. Zip and bar codes, and Morse code as well, are good examples of digital innovations in the service of our analog activity. E-ZPass is another example of the digital serving our analog needs for more rapid car travel. There are also many new digital technologies in medicine that serve the human body well. Perhaps the very first was the digital thermometer; there have been a great many since then.

Integration of Analog and Digital

Integration is more than cooperation, since it requires the mutual interaction of the two modes so as to bring about important and new understanding that neither mode could provide by itself. Here are examples from science: Isaac Newton's physics involved the mapping of a digital mathematics onto analog observations. In addition, the calculus itself involved the link of the digital to high-level analogs of area and slope.[156] The same is true for Albert Einstein's equations, which were also mapped into empirical observations. In fact, all valid scientific theory seems to involve this integration, or connection, of digital mathematical abstraction and analog observed data.

Even significant mathematics is also a connection of numerical symbols to an underlying implicit visual geometry. For example, in their book, *Where Mathematics Come From,* George Lakoff and Rafael Nunez clearly show that embodied mental concepts underlie mathematics and bring it into being. They provide good evidence that abstract mathematical ideas arise via metaphor coming from the way we function in the everyday physical world.

Similarly, architecture involves abstract visual ideas that are mapped into drawings and then into bricks, physical columns, beams, stones, and shingles. Apparently new creative ideas involve the mapping or connecting of an abstract mental representation into a concrete perceptual reality. It is reasonable to propose that creativity is always a mapping or connection between some abstract digital code or idea and some observable analog reality.

Here then is a summary of how to address the problem of digital imperialism: first is tolerance between the two positions and those who represent them, then cooperation between each position, and finally integration of analog and digital, with the digital leading the way but always in the service of the analog.

But is this possible? The question arises: is anything like cooperation, much less integration, likely to take place today with the present huge divide between the two cultures?

Chapter 10
HOW ANALOG AND DIGITAL INTEGRATION
CAN OCCUR

Let us look at two cases where a recovery and new integration have occurred in the arts. This can give us hope for the future: a more fundamental recovery of the real is possible in the culture at large, and in particular a return to a "mature" religion, one that has gone through the fire of modernity. (More on this later.)

Classical Music:
From Modernist Theory to a Return to Tonality

In the early 1900s, classical music moved decisively away from traditional tonality and harmony to an increasingly abstract expression of compositional logics unrelated to our normal emotional responses. This movement was led by Arnold Schoenberg with later help from Anton Webern and Pierre Boulez. These composers rejected the premise that music was governed by natural relationships; they believed that music could be defined by man and that it was without necessary natural properties. For example, they assumed that tonality was an unnecessary human convention. Their atonal music had no key or center, and the principle of dodecaphony treated the twelve tones of our scale as all equally important. In such works, each tone had to occur before any tone could be repeated. (This is a familiar digital emphasis—the rejection of natural differences by emphasizing equality.) This kind of modernist, abstract, theoretical approach dominated classical music until around the 1970s.

But, however interesting these theoretical compositions were to the composers who wrote them, as music they sounded like painful cacophony to most listeners. The composers and music theorist and critics who advocated dodecaphony and atonal music controlled much of the music world for decades; they were contemptuous and harsh in their response to any who objected. (This is another example of interpersonal digital/left hemisphere imperialism.) They thought they were a new avant garde waiting for the audience to catch up. However, after many years of trying to get accepted, the movement failed; it seems to have more or less died out. I propose that this music was a good example of a highly digital or left-brain music that had turned its back on right-hemisphere responses. The digital was put in the service of itself.

Around 1980 classical music began its return to tonality, and melody, rhythm, and harmony—first in a tentative way through the minimal music of Philip Glass, Steve Reich, and others, and then through what can be called the neo-traditional music of Heinrich Gorecki, John Tavener, and Arvo Pärt. Many other composers soon joined in this recovery. Today neo-classical composers are common—and with them we enjoy a return to the beautiful in the world of classical music. (Listen, for example, to Sir James MacMillan's Fifth symphony.)

Painting:
From Modernism and Postmodernism Back to Beauty

"Modernist" art is a more precise term for what most people think of as modern art. Modernist art began in France around 1860 with Edouard Manet and soon developed into a form called Impressionism, a colorful, rather blurry realism that removed much depth from its representation of the world. But it was certainly beautiful, and it is loved by many. Around 1900 modernist art moved into a schematic period with still less depth, perhaps best remembered in the work of Pablo Picasso with his fauve nudes. Shortly afterwards modernist painting moved to an abstract geometry with no reference to recognizable objects. This was expressed in the paintings of Robert Delaunay, Wassily Kandinsky, and Piet Mondrian's linear abstractions. This kind of expression dominated more or less until the 1950s. Then even simple geometric shapes were no longer especially innovative. Instead, we got the completely abstract drip paintings, with no depth, by Jackson Pollock and the homogeneous color fields of Mark Rothko and others. Then came entirely homogeneous paintings, such as those by Robert Irwin.

Abstraction now no longer allowed even different colors or lines on the canvas. Irwin's all-white gallery wall, actually made of white scrim material, invisible as a piece of art, was now almost the end of modernism. The actual last stage of modernist painting came with conceptual art about the year 1970. Conceptual art proposed that there should not be any physical art object at all, just an idea. This was fully digital, total left-hemisphere art. One example is an image of the word: idea—but, in theory there should not even be this physical object or image. This understanding of visual art was powerfully critiqued in a book by the well-known writer, Tom Wolfe, titled "The Painted Word."[157] It's his insightful interpretation of how modernist art, which from the beginning had needed theory, that is, words, to explain itself had now ended in just words.

Wolfe's interpretation had been anticipated years earlier by Ortega y Gasset,[158] who characterized modernist art as a movement that progressively eliminated the human; human content became negligible. Gasset claimed that this type of art avoided living forms, that it was just ironical, and even that it explicitly claimed to have no transcendent meaning.

The modernist movement, culminating in extreme abstraction and conceptual art, was followed by a return to the image in a period usually termed postmodern. This began in the 1960s with the early images of Andy Warhol featuring Marilyn Monroe, Campbell's soup cans, Roy Lichtenstein's comic strip works, and other enlarged paintings of popular images. The initial tone was rather humorous and positive. Soon, however, postmodern art slid into satire and irony—into rejection of the Western tradition of beauty and higher or transcendent meaning. It was the "paint the moustache on the Mona Lisa" period. Now it was fine to use elephant dung to paint the Virgin Mary; or to put Jesus, as a crucifix, in a container of urine; to make a sculpture of an enormously large ashtray filled with big cigarette butts; or to place the skinned heads of cows in pristine glass boxes titled "the 12 apostles."

But, at present, after some 30 or 40 years, postmodern art seems to have ended in the early 2000s. The ending of modernist and postmodernist painting has taken place quietly; both seem to have died with a whimper, not a bang. Although good realist painting existed in a somewhat underground form in the first three-quarters of the twentieth century, it is now a strong and major movement with many important artists returning to nature and to beauty.[159]

In light of this recovery of tonality in music and of beauty in contemporary painting there is hope for a genuine return to human-based meaning in the arts, and thus for the culture as a whole.

The ongoing popularity of films throughout both the modernist and postmodern periods is also a sign of hope. Film has always kept to the image, and to meaningful interpersonal relationships, and has often presented physical and natural beauty. In short, film has remained both popular and richly analog.

A Return to Mature Religion as a Positive Way Forward

As a short reminder, let us look briefly at how destructive modernism has been to the culture at large. A critical retrospective of the individuals responsible for many of the more recent forms of modernity is summarized in Paul Johnson's *Intellectuals: From Marx and Tolstoy to Sartre and Chomsky*. The ending of this trajectory is captured in Roger Scruton's *Fools, Frauds, and Firebrands: Thinkers of the New Left*.[160] Scruton also shows what I believe is obvious to many—that all these modern or postmodern preoccupations show signs of fatigue; they have become clichés. "The herd of Independent People" and their interpretations and proposals for what is new or radical are now part of an exhausted establishment.

We are ready for a new historical period, one much more focused on, let me suggest, adult or grown-up issues. A more adult-focused era would recover religion, but religion purged of superstition and other harmful characteristics, thanks to the critiques of modernism. Religion that has gone through the fire of modernism can be called "mature."

In this new adult era, there would be proportionally fewer children combined with a declining population. Moreover, the coming average older age of the population will lessen the interest in sex and rebellion. One already existing example of this is the growth of effective, organized hostility to pornography. There are other signs of such changes, including the many returns to reality, plus the drift of population from the cities to smaller, localized communities.

Such a new type of society would require big social changes that seem unlikely to take place by rational planning or from existing political or social forces. More likely, it requires the end, presumably by wasting away or by destruction, of the present large systems. These systems can slowly disintegrate, but there are a number of possible destructive "black swans" that could do this quickly. Examples include nuclear war, a more lethal virus-based pandemic than COVID-19, or a financial collapse. Some people would include the effects of climate change and even "end times" disasters. Given any such an event, or combination of such events, the point is to have a new plan with which to respond in a positive way to the ensuing chaos.

A positive plan will involve many of the more analog economic and social structures mentioned earlier under the return to the real. Such a return would not be a kind of new ideology; after all, ideological language is very digital. A return to a new form of integrated analog and digital social characteristics could be developed in different ways across any large geographic area and would be highly influenced by the different histories of the location in which they took place.

Besides the possible responses already described, I suggest a return to mature religion as part of a contemporary answer to the present search for identity and higher meaning, as a resolution for the need for a moral framework, and as a way to leave behind our present world, which is so individualistic that we don't really care for others.

The Case for Mature Religion: The Digital in the Service of the Analog

Each of the religions discussed below brings a clear higher meaning to each believer, along with a moral framework and an involvement with and a concern for other persons. All of these religions have gone through the refining fire of modernity, thus their maturity. My focus is on how they involve the integration of analog and digital characteristics of religious life.

Jewish Life and Worship

What are the digital aspects of Judaism? The basic answer is obvious: The Scriptures. For thousands of years, the Jews have continued to discuss, debate, and sometimes separate into different groups over the interpretation of Scripture. The digital life has been strong and remains so to this day.

As to the analog aspects of Judaism, perhaps they become especially obvious with Moses and the story of Exodus. After marking their doors, the Jewish people escape from Egypt through the Red Sea. Moses brings down from the mountain the Tablets of the Ten Commandments given by God. The Jews then succeed in establishing themselves, with God's help, in the Promised Land, and the prophets continue their personal contact with God. The Jewish people either listen to and worship God or turn away from Him. In this history God is connected, is covenanted, to them in very physical ways. This is all very analog. The importance of revelation for the Jews is that it is a clear example of real events and real contacts with God, who is otherwise invisible and abstract.

In addition, Jewish meals like preparing and eating the Seder meal, wearing a skullcap (yarmulkes), going to synagogue, avoiding pork and other non-kosher food, all clearly demonstrate analog religious life. The Jews have been called "the people of the body."[161]

Protestant Life and Worship

For serious Protestants digital involvement is obvious in their emphasis on the Bible, and on the importance given to the sermon. Theological debate and disputes have been at the origin of many new denominations and continue as a lively presence of the digital throughout Protestantism.

And their analog religious life? Protestants first and foremost have produced many hymns of great beauty. Hymn singing has been and remains an important part of Protestant worship. Today many Catholic services use these originally Protestant hymns. A second analog emphasis is the church social, for example, church picnics. Protestants have pioneered many religious and social activities after services and during the week, such as Bible reading groups. Other Protestant analog activities include having total immersion baptisms, not working on Sunday, and not drinking alcohol. Of course, the many charismatic and Pentecostal services demonstrate very analog forms of Protestant worship. (So once did the Quakers and the Shakers.) And again, these charismatic behaviors are integrated with an interpretation of Scripture, the digital.

Catholic and Orthodox Life and Worship

Both the digital and analog characteristics of Catholic worship are clear; the same kind of analog and digital understanding is similar for the Eastern Orthodox Church.

The digital emphasis on Scripture is strong, though perhaps less so than in Protestantism. The Catholic Magisterium with its official catechism of the faith is another digital example, as are the many papal encyclicals. One recent important papal document, which shows the combination of digital with analog, is the widely influential "Theology of the Body" by St. John Paul II, with its celebration of the human body in theological terms.

Within the Catholic Liturgy, the first part of the Mass focuses more on the digital, with an Old Testament, New Testament, and then a Gospel reading, followed by the homily and the Creed. This first part is called "The Liturgy of the Word." The second and most important part of the Mass focuses on the analog, in "The Liturgy of the Eucharist." Here worshipers kneel, they stand, they respond to the words pronounced by the priest, they give the peace sign to others nearby—and, most important, they eat the host and may drink the wine. The very center of the Mass is the "Real Presence of Christ" in the host. Catholics also venerate the crucifix showing the body of Christ, they cross themselves, they use holy water. All these are obvious Catholic analog activities.

Because Christianity involves the integration of analog and digital and because it has been so involved in the history of the West, Christianity cannot accept either extreme analog, that is, right-wing, or extreme digital, that is, left-wing, political positions. At any particular time and place, it may lean against the dominant position, but Christianity thoroughly rejects both racism and ideology.

Finally, recall that creativity is the linking of the concrete analog with the abstract digital. For Christians this is best summarized in God's great creative act: The Word was made Flesh. In this expression lies the answer to a person's identity. Discover a true identity through the adventure of seeking it in your response to God.

ENDNOTES

1   Claire McCarthy, "Anxiety in Teens is Rising: What's Going On?," *Healthy Chil-dren.org*, November 20, 2019. Also increasing in the young are depression and suicide. See, for example, https://www.breitbart.com/health/2023/02/15/cdc-57-of-teen-girls-feel-sad-hopeless-24-made-plans-for-suicide/. CDC data show 57% of teen girls feel sad, depressed, hopeless; 24% made plans for suicide. Accessed 2.16.2023.

2   "The State of Mental Health in America," *Mental Health America*, https://mhanational.org › issues › state-mental-health-america.
    Youth mental health is worsening. 9.7% of youth in the U.S. have severe major depression, compared to 9.2% in last year's dataset. This rate was highest among youth who identify as more than one race, at 12.4%. [[instead of "last year", perhaps give the date?]] Even before COVID-19, the prevalence of mental illness among adults was increasing. In 2017–2018, 19% of adults experienced a mental illness, an increase of 1.5 million people over the previous year's dataset. Suicidal ideation among adults is increasing. The percentage of adults in the U.S. who are experiencing serious thoughts of suicide increased 0.15% from 2016–2017 to 2017–2018—an additional 460,000 people . https://mhanational.org/issues/state-mental-health-america; (2018). CDC data show U.S. life expectancy continues to decline with suicide, drug overdose deaths named as key contributors. https://www.aafp.org/news/health-of-the public/20181210lifeexpectdrop.html+.

3   Winston Churchill, "Fifty Years Hence, 1931," speech delivered December, 1931, *America's National Churchill Museum*, https://www.nationalchurchill-museum.org/fifty-years-hence.html.

4   Aldous Huxley, *Brave New World* (New York: Harper Perennial, 1932); Jacques Ellul, *The Technological Society*, trans. John Wilkinson (New York: Vintage, 1964); Ellul, *The Technological Bluff*, trans. Geoffrey W. Bromily (Grand Rapids, MI: Eerdmans, 1990); Jurgen Habermas, *Technology and Science as "Ideology"*, 3rd ed. (Frankfurt: Suhrkamp Verlag, 1969); Neil Postman, *Technopoly: The Surrender of Culture to Technology* (New York: Vintage, 1993); Wendell Berry, *The Unsettling of America* (San Francisco: Sierra Club Books, 1977); Robert N. Bellah, *Habits of the Heart* (New York: Harper Collins, 1985); Charles Taylor, *The Ethics of Authenticity* (Cambridge, MA: Harvard University Press, 1991); Martin Rees, *Our Final Hour: A Scientist's Warning;*

How Terror, Error, and Environmental Disaster Threaten Humankind's Future in This Century—On Earth and Beyond (New York: Basic Books, 2003).

5   Taylor, *The Ethics of Authenticity.*

6   M. C. Henrie, review of *The Ethics of* Authenticity, by Charles Taylor, *Chronicles,* September 1993, p. 33. Much of my summary is taken from Mark Henrie's review of Taylor's book.

7   See Charles Pierce in William P. Alston, "Meaning," in *The Encyclopedia of Philosophy,* ed. Paul Edwards (New York, NY: Macmillan, 1967); Ernest Cassirer, *The Philosophy of Symbolic Forms* (New Haven, CT: Yale University Press, 1952); Suzanne K. Langer, *Philosophy in a New Key* (Cambridge, MA: Harvard University Press, 1943); Anthony Wilden, "Analog and Digital Communication: On the Relationship between Negation, Signification, and the Emergence of the Discrete Element," *Semiotica* 6 (1972): 50–82; also, Paul Watzlawick, Janet H. Beavin, & Don Jackson, *Pragmatics of Human Communication* (New York, NY: Norton, 1967). Within psychology, a former colleague of mine, Donald Spence, has an early but still relevant treatment of analog and digital modes of communication. "Analog and Digital Descriptions of Behavior," *American Psychologist* 28, no. 6 (1973): 479–88, https://doi.org/10.1037/h0034998. Early aspects of this distinction in our experience of the world can be found in the work of Arthur Schopenhauer, first published in 1819, *Die Welt als Wille und Vorstellung,* trans. E. F. Payne as *The World as Will and Representation* (New York: Dover, 1966), and in the works of Henri Bergson, first in his 1896 work, *Essai sur les données immediates de la conscience,* trans. F. L. Pogson as *Time and Freewill* (London: Allen and Unwin, 1910), and then again in Bergson, *Matiere et Memoire,* trans N. M. Paul and W. S. Palmer as *Matter and Memory* (London: Allen and Unwin, 1911.) The work of these two philosphers was brought to my attention by J. C. Cutting, *Principles of Psychopathology: Two Worlds, Two Minds, Two Hemispheres* (Oxford: Oxford University Press, 1997).

8   Wilden, "Analog and Digital Communication," 56–58; see also P. Watzlawick, J. H. Beavin, and D. D. Jackson, *Pragmatics of Human Communication* (New York: Norton, 1967), 61, 65.

9   Allan Paivio, *Imagery and Verbal Processes* (New York: Holt, Rinehart, and Winston, 1971). Paivio, *Mental Representations: A Dual Coding Approach* (Oxford: Oxford University Press, 1971).

10   Wilden, "Analog and Digital Communication," 58.

11   It is quite possible that the long conflict in philosophy often called the "one vs. the many" is a consequence of the qualitative difference between analog and digital codes and the two brain hemispheres; the right brain, or analog, and left brain, or digital, that underly the codes.

12   Daryl Cooper, *Digital Disaster,* review of *Human Forever: The Digital Politics of Spiritual War,* by James Poulos. Canonic. In *Claremont Review of Books* 22, no. 3, Summer 2022, p. 77.

13 Nathan Adlen, "The Truth Revealed: Are Old Trucks Better Than New? Mr. Truck With 60 Years of Knowledge Tells ALL!" *TFLTruck*, April 12, 2021, https://tfltruck.com/2021/04/the-truth-revealed-are-old-trucks-better-than-new-mr-truck-with-60-years-of-knowledge-tells-all/.

14 L. A. Riggs, F. Ratliff, J. C. Cornsweet, T. N. Cornsweet, "The Disappearance of Steadily Fixated Visual Test Objects," *Journal of the Optical Society of America* 43, no. 6 (1953): 495–501. https://doi.org/10.1364/JOSA.43.000495.

15 Walter Ong, *The Presence of the Word: Some Prolegomena for Cultural and Religious History* (New Haven, CT: Yale University Press, 1967); Ong, *Interfaces of the Word: Studies in the Evolution of Consciousness and Culture* (Ithaca, NY: Cornell University Press, 1977); also, Ong, *Orality & Literacy: The Technologizing of the Word* (London: Routledge, 1988).

16 Ong, *Orality & Literacy*, 31–73, 78.

17 Ong, *The Presence of the Word*, 111.

18 Ong, *The Presence of the Word*, 283.

19 Ong, *Interfaces of the Word*, 21.

20 Ong, *Interfaces of the Word*, 136.

21 Ong, *Interfaces of the Word*, 136–7.

22 Ong, *Interfaces of the Word*, 256.

23 Ong, *Interfaces of the Word*, 17.

24 Ong, *Interfaces of the Word*, 18.

25 See McGilchrist, *The Master and His Emissary: The Divided Brain and the Making of the Western World* (New Haven, CT: Yale University Press, 2009).

26 V. D. Hanson, 2021. Victor Davis Hanson: "The 'Credentialed Class'" *Fox News*, https://www.foxnews.com › media › victor-davis-hanson-.

27 Thomas Merton, *The Waters of Siloe* (New York: Harcourt Brace, 1949), 283.

28 Merton, *The Waters of Siloe*, 283–84.

29 L. E. Lehrman, "The Demise of Money and Credit." *The American Spectator*, May 2013, http://spectator.org/archives/2013/05/30/the-demise-of-money-and/credit/.

30 P. Hanks, k. Hardcastle, and F. Hodges, *Dictionary of First Names*, 2nd ed. (Oxford: Oxford University Press, 2006).

31 See C. T. Onions, (*The Oxford Dictionary of English Oetymology* (Oxford: Oxford University Press, 1966). See also J. Ayto, *Dictionary of Word Origins* (New York, NY: Arcade, 2011).

32 See David Diringer, David Olsen, et al., "Alphabet: Definition, History, & Facts," *Britannica*, July 18, 2024, https://www.britannica.com › ... and History of the alphabet. Also see, F. I. Andersen and D. N. Freedman, D. N. (1989), "Aleph as a Vowel Letter in Old Aramaic," in *To Touch the Text: Biblical and Related Studies in Honor of Joseph A. Fitzmyer S.J.*, ed. Maurya P. Horgan and Paul J. Kobelski (New York: Crossroads, 1989), 3–14.

33 See "Alphabet (Early Greek)," course material posted online from the

Joukowsky Institute for Archaeology & the Ancient World, at Brown University, https://www.brown.edu/Departments/Joukowsky_Institute/courses/greek-past/4739.html.

34 *Wall Street Journal*, Dec. 6, 1991, B-1. B-9. B-12.

35 Y. Mochizuki & S. Shinomoto, November, 2013. "Analog and digital codes in the brain." *Physical Review, 89(*2),1-10. DOI: 10.1103/PhysRevE.89.022705

36 Vitz, P.C.(1983) The brain hemispheres and human response to art. In *Human Responses to Art*, by C. Seerveld and P. C. Vitz, . Dordt College Press, 19-44. Vitz, P. C. (1988). "Analog and digital art: A brain hemisphere critique of modern painting." In F. H. Farley and R. W. Neperud (eds.) *The Foundations of Aesthetics, Art & Art Education*. New York, NY: Praeger. 43–86; Vitz, P. C. (1990). The use of stories in moral development: New psychological reasons for an old education method. *American Psychologist*, 45, 709–720.

37 McGilchrist, I. (2009*). The Master and his Emissary: The Divided Brain and the Making of the Western World*. New Haven, CT: Yale University Press. The idea that Western culture is dominated by the left brain goes back at least to Marshall McLuhan, 1978, where he wrote "the Western world remains dominated by the left-brain hemisphere…" p. 34, in "The Brain and the Media: The Western Hemisphere." *Journal of Communication, 28,* 34–40.

38 McGilchrist, I. (2009), chapter 1; McGilchrist, 2012, kindle, REF?18%-19%; Galaburda, A. M. (1995). "Anatomic basis of cerebral dominance." In R. J. Davidson & K. Hugdahl (es.), *Brain Asymmetry* (pp. 51–73). Cambridge, MA: MIT Press.

39 McGilchrist, 2009, chapter 2.

40 Kinsbourne, M. (1982). "Hemispheric specialization and the growth of human understanding." *American Psychologist, 37(*4), 411–20. https://doi.org/10.1037/0003-066X.37.4.411 Kinsbourne, M. (1988). "Integrated field theory of consciousness." In A. J. Marcel & E. Bisiach (eds.), *Consciousness in Contemporary Science* (pp. 239–56). Clarendon Press/Oxford University Press. Federmeier, K. & Kutas, M. (1999). "Right words and left words: electrophysiological evidence for hemisphere differences in memory processing." *Cognitive Brain Research,8,* (3), 373–92.

41 Sackeim, H. A., Greenberg, M. S., Weiman, A. L., Gur, R. C., Hungerbuhler, J.P., & Geschwind , N. (1982). "Hemispheric asymmetry in the expression of positive and negative emotions." *Neurologic Evidence.* 39(4):210–18. doi: 10.1001/archneur.1982.00510160016003. Also, Davidson, R. J. (1995). "Cerebral asymmetry, emotion, and affective style." In R. J. Davidson & K. Hugdahl (eds.), *Brain Asymmetry* (pp. 361–87). Cambridge, MA: MIT Press.

42 McGilchrist, 2009, p. 209.

43 McGilchrist, 2009, p. 209.

44 Gonzalez, J. & McLennan, C.T. (2009). "Hemisphere differences in the recognition of environmental sounds." https://doi.org/10.1111/j.1467-9280.2009.02379.x; Tervaniemi, M. & Hugdahl, K. (2003). "Lateralization of auditory-cortex functions." *Brain Research Reviews 43*(3), 231–46.

45 McGilchrist, 2010. "Reciprocal organization of the cerebral hemispheres." *Dialogues in Clinical Neuroscience, 12(*4), 503–15, p. 504.

46 McGilchrist, (2012). *The Divided Brain and the Search for Meaning.* kindle 30%, Kindle location 133.

47 McGilchrist, 2009, p. 33.

48 See Vitz, (2017). "The origin of consciousness in the integration of analog (right hemisphere) & digital (left hemisphere) codes." *Journal of Consciousness Exploration & Research, 8*(11), pp. 881–906.

49 Tervaniemi, M. & Hugdahl, K. (2003). "Lateralization of auditory-cortex functions." *Brain Research Rev*iew *Dec;43*(3):231–46. doi: 10.1016/j.brainresrev.2003.08.004.

50 McGilchrist, 2012, kindle 56%, Kindle loc 271.

51 Gazzaniga, M. S. & LeDoux, J. E. (1978). *The Integrated Mind.* New York, NY: Plenum. p.72.

52 McGilchrist, 2012, kindle, 74%, loc. 351.

53 Goldin-Meadow, S. & Beilock, S. L. (2010) "Action's influence on thought: The case of gesture." https://doi.org/10.1177/1745691610388764.

54 McGilchrist, 2012. Kindle Location 134.

55 McGilchrist, McGilchrist, 2012. Kindle Location 133.

56 McGilchrist, McGilchrist, 2012. Kindle Location 129.

57 McGilchrist, McGilchrist, 2012. Kindle Location 155.

58 McGilchrist, McGilchrist, 2012. Kindle Location 198.

59 McGilchrist, McGilchrist, 2012. Kindle Location 203.

60 McGilchrist, McGilchrist, 2012. Kindle Location 219.

61 McGilchrist, McGilchrist, 2012. Kindle Location 255.

62 McGilchrist, McGilchrist, 2012. Kindle Location 267.

63 McGilchrist, McGilchrist, 2012. Kindle Location 267.

64 From McGilchrist, *The Master and His Emissary* and *The Divided Brain and the Search for Meaning.*

65 Oscar Wilde, *Lady Windermere's Fan,* act 3.

66 S. Baron-Cohen, *The Essential Difference: Male and Female Brains and the Truth About Autism* (New York: Basic Books, 2003).

67 Baron-Cohen, *The Essential Difference,* 91.

68 Baron-Cohen, *The Essential Difference,* 92.

69 Baron-Cohen. *The Essential Difference,* 7, 149–53.

70 P. Belluck, "Oxytocin Found to Stimulate Social Brain Regions in Children with Autism," *New York Times,* Dec. 2, 2013, A18, https://www.nytimes.com/2013/12/03/health/-oxytocin-found-to-stimulate-brain-children-with-autism.html.

71 McGilchrist, *The Master and His Emissary,* 3.

72 See notes 3 and 4 in the introduction; also see McGilchrist, *The Master and His Emissary* and *The Divided Brain and the Search for Meaning.*

73 A. Giddens, *Modernity and Self-identity: Self and Society in the Late Modern Age* (Stanford, CA: Stanford University Press, 1991), 39, 90.

74 Lucy Waterlow, "It's a Way to Escape," *Daily Mail*, May 24, 2016, http://www.dailymail.co.uk/femail/article-3604744/Graduates-CEOs-reveal-addicted-dressing-DOGS.html; N. Golgowski, "Meet Eric, 22, Who Lives Life as a Merman…," *Daily Mail*, April 2, 2013, http://www.dailymail.co.uk/news/article-2303161/Eric-Ducharme-Meet-man-lives-life-merman-Florida-natural-springs.html; S. Brennan, "'I Was Born in the Wrong Species': Woman Who Says She's a Cat…," *Daily Mail*, January 2016, http//www.dailymail.co.uk/femail/article-3419631/Woman-says-she-s-CAT-trapped-human-body.html; "Police Appeal over Half-Naked, Web-Footed Mystery Woman Claiming to be 'Mermaid,'" News.au.com, April 7, 2017, http//www.news.com.au/lifestyle/real-life/wtf/pe0olice-appeal-over-halfnaked-webfooted-mystery-woman-claiming-to-be-mermaid/news-story/8d7ca6e0de31b9a0a5tc; C. Burns, "Horsing Around. This Woman Lives as Horse Every Day…," *The Sun*, November 2016, https://www.thesun.co.uk/living/2209477/this-woman-lived-as-horse-every-day-for-seven-years-by-trotting-on-all-fours-and-eating-grass/; *Hooked on the Look*, "I Went from Hotshot Banker to Genderless Reptile …," videography by Davin Fitch; produced by Erin Cardiff and Kim Nguyen, edited by Pete Ansell, July 7, 2021, https://www.youtube.com/watch?v=e9HxE4ROUvM; Will Grice, "Birdman of Bristol," *The Sun*, July 8, 2016, The.sun.co.uk/living/1406536/meet-the-man-whos-so-obsessed-with-looking-like-a-parrot-he-changed-his-name-to-ted-parrotman-and-cut-off-his-own-ears/.

75 See Casey Shutt, letter, *First Things,* March 2023, no. 331, p. 4.

76 Alice Walker, "Jailhouse Tot," *The U.S. Sun*, April 9, 2022, https://www.the-sun.com/news/world-news/5090044/trans-killer-identifying-baby-scots-prison/.

77 Elves and dragons and faeries, oh my!, "Various theories and the like…The otherkin community," *Ever Awakening to Ourselves* (live journal), Otherkin website, https;//otherkin.livejournal.com/30114.html; T. Windtree, "What Are Otherkin?," Otherkin website, Sept. 10, 2016, https://www.otherkin.net/2016/09/what-are-otherkin/.

78 "Elves and Brownies," The Silver Elves Blog, Sept. 15, 2009. https://silverelves.wordpress.com/2009/09/15/.

79 Riley Black, "I'm a Furry. Netflix's *Sexy Beasts* Misses the Entire Point of Dressing Up Like an Animal," Slate, July, 22, 2021, https://slate.com/human-interest/2021/07/furry-sexy-beasts-costumes-netflix-mistakes.html.

80 Mark Bauerlein, "How Digital Youth Became Unhappy—and Dangerous—Adults," *First Things*, February 1, 2022; all quotes from *First Things*. Excerpted and adapted from Mark Bauerlein, *The Dumbest Generation Grows Up from Stupefied Youth to Dangerous Adults* (Washington, DC: Regnery Gateway, 2022).

81 D. Glidden, W. P. Bouman, B. A. , and J. Arcelus, "Gender Dysphoria and Autism Spectrum Disorder: A Systematic Review of the Literature," *Sexual Medicine Reviews* 4 no. 1 (2016): 3–14.

82 A third contributor can be sexual or physical abuse, which, in the case of girls, can make their own sex seem weak and create a desire to identify with maleness as something that is strong. Author's clinical experience.

83 G. K. Chesterton, "Three Foes of the Family," in *The Common Man*.

84 David Bromwich, "'Have Democrats Become the Party of the Rich?," *The Nation*, September 6, 2021, https://www.thenation.com/article/society/democrats-rich-party-obama/.

85 Robert Bellah, *Habits of the Heart: Individualism and Commitment in American Life* (Berkeley, CA: University of California Press, 1996). This new left-brain world is abstract and removed from fellow-feeling; it is utilitarian in ethics; over-confident of its view of reality.

86 McGilchrist, *The Master and His Emissary*, especially chapter 6.

87 NPR. Lyft and Uber will pay drivers' legal fees if they're sued under Texas abortion law. The CEO of each company, Logan Green of Lyft and Dara Khosrowshahi of Uber, supported giving money to Planned Parenthood and criticized the Texas law. Npr.org/2021/09/03/103414080/lyft-and-uber-will-pay-drivers'-legal-fees-if-theyre-sued-under-texas-abortion-law.

88 Samuel T. Francis, see *Chronicles*, April, 2005; for Murray see Herrenstein, R. and Murray, C. (1996). *The Bell Curve: Intelligence and Class Structure in America*. New York, NY: Free Press: Simon & Schuster.

89 See George Soros, Wikipedia, for this well-known fact. https://en.wikipedia.org/wiki/George_Soros.

90 Hanson, Victor Davis July 15, 2021, *PJ Media*, "Democratic party won't admit it's become the party of wealth." https://pjmedia.com/victordavishanson/2021/07/15/democratic-party-wont-admit-its-become-the-party-of-wealth-n1461967; Bromwich, D. (Sept. 6, 2021) "Have democrats become the party of the rich." *The Nation,* https://www.thenation.com/article/society/democrats-rich-party-obama/.

91 Kotkin, J., (2021). "Economic civil war." *The American Mind.* p. 1, 5, Salvo 02.23.2021. https://american mind.org/salvo/economic-civil-war/.

92 Kotkin, J. (2020). *The coming of neo-feudalism.* Encounter Books, NY.

93 Green, D. (2021), *The Spectator,* February, US edition.

94 Thomas Molnar, *Chronicles,* Feb.1988, p.14, 15; David Levy, *The World & I,* Feb.1987.

95 Sahu, M., Ghandi, S. & Sharma, M. K. (Oct./Dec. 2019). "Mobile phone addiction among children and adolescents: A systematic review." *Journal Addictions Nursing,* 2019, *30*(4) 261–68.

96 Elaine Mead, "Does Your Phone Give You Anxiety? 7 Steps to Cope," Healthline, Aug 13, 2020, https://www.healthline.com/health/does-your-phone-give-you-

anxiety-7-steps-to-cope: "Phone anxiety happens when we turn to our phones as a form of distraction. They can even be an escape from anxious feelings in other areas of our lives." ABC News, "Excessive cellphone Use May Cause Anxiety, Experts Warn," *ABC News* Jul 28, 2017, https://abcnews.go.com/Lifestyle/excessive-cellphone-anxiety-experts-warn/story?id=48842476: "'If you're constantly connected, you're going to feel anxiety,' researcher says." Susan Davis, "Addicted to Your Smartphone? Here's What to Do," WebMD, June 20, 2012, https://www.webmd.com/balance/features/addicted-your-smartphone-what-to-do.

97 Sehar Shoukat, "CellPhone Addiction and Psychological and Physiological Health in Adolescents," *Experimental and Clinical Sciences Journal* 18 (2019): 47–50, does a good job of summarizing the iPhone pathology. See the letter for cellphone usage and for summaries of research references; e.g., Seong-Soo Cha and Bo-Kyung Seo, "Smartphone Use and Smartphone Addiction in Middle School Students in Korea: Prevalence, Social Networking Service, and Game Use," *Health Psychology Open* 5, no. 1 (2018): 2055102918755046.

98 Tessa Jones, "Students' Cell Phone Addiction and Their Opinions," *The Elon Journal of Undergraduate Research in Communications* 5, no. 1 (2014): 74–80., cited in Shoukat, "Cell Phone Addiction."

99 Anna Schoeni, Katharina Roser, and Martin Röösli, "Symptoms and Cognitive Functions in Adolescents in Relation to Mobile Phone Use During Night," *PloS one* 10, no. 7 (2015): e0133528, cited in Shoukat, "Cell Phone Addiction."

100 Leonard Reinecke, Stefan Aufenanger, Manfred E. Beutel, Michael Dreier, Oliver Quiring, Birgit Stark, Klaus Wölfling, and Kai W. Müller, "Digital Stress over the Life Span: The Effects of Communication Load and Internet Multitasking on Perceived Stress and Psychological Health Impairments in a German Probability Sample," *Media Psychology* 20, no. 1 (2017): 90–115, cited in Shoukat, "Cell Phone Addiction."

101 Jocelyne Matar Boumosleh and Doris Jaalouk, "Depression, Anxiety, and Smartphone Addiction in University Students—A Cross Sectional Study," *PloS one* 12, no. 8 (2017): e0182239, cited in Shoukat, "Cell Phone Addiction."

102 S. J. Brian, "Two Days with No Phone," *Scholastic Action* 37 (2013): 4–6., cited in Shoukat, "Cell Phone Addiction."

103 Siew Foen Ng, Nor Syamimi Illiani Che Hassan, Nor Hairunnisa Mohammad Nor, and Nur Ain Abdul Malek, "The Relationship between Smartphone Use and Academic Performance: A Case of Students in A Malaysian Tertiary Institution," *Malaysian Online Journal of Educational Technology* 5, no. 4 (2017): 58–70; Stijn Baert, Sunčica Vujić, Simon Amez, Matteo Claeskens, Thomas Daman, Arno Maeckelberghe, Eddy Omey, and Lieven De Marez, "Smartphone Use and Academic Performance: Correlation or Causal Relationship?,"

Kyklos 73, no. 1 (2020): 22–46.; Andrew Lepp, Jacob E. Barkley, and Aryn C. Karpinski, "The Relationship between Cell Phone Use and Academic Performance in a Sample of US College Students," *Sage Open* 5, no. 1 (2015): 2158244015573169; Jocelyne Boumosleh and Doris Jaalouk, "Smartphone Addiction among University Students and its Relationship with Academic Performance," *Global Journal of Health Science* 10, no. 1 (2018): 48–59; all cited in Shoukat, "Cell Phone Addiction."

104 K. S. Negi and S. Godiyal, "College Students' Opinion about Cell Phone Usage," *Int Educ Sci Res J* 2, no. 10 (2016): 35–38, cited in Shoukat, "Cell Phone Addiction."

105 Sara Thomée, Annika Härenstam, and Mats Hagberg, "Mobile Phone Use and Stress, Sleep Disturbances, and Symptoms of Depression among Young Adults—A Prospective Cohort Study," *BMC Public Health* 11 (2011): 1–11, cited in Shoukat, "Cell Phone Addiction."

106 José De-Sola Gutiérrez, Fernando Rodríguez de Fonseca, and Gabriel Rubio, "Cell-Phone Addiction: A Review," *Frontiers in Psychiatry* 7 (2016): 175, cited in Shoukat, "Cell Phone Addiction."

107 Cha and Seo, "Smartphone Use and Smartphone Addiction in Middle School Students in Korea," cited in Shoukat, "Cell Phone Addiction."

108 Christoph Augner and Gerhard W. Hacker, "Associations between Problematic Mobile Phone Use and Psychological Parameters in Young Adults," *International Journal of Public Health* 57 (2012): 437–41, cited in Shoukat, "Cell Phone Addiction."

109 Another possible interpretation is that there is an indirect relation between cellphone usage and psychological health. Using cellphones at night leads to insomnia, and lack of sleep ultimately results in anxiety and depression. And, of course, both explanations could be correct, either working together or separately for different individuals. Shoukat, "Cell Phone Addiction."

110 C. Olvera, G. T. Stebbins, C. G. Goetz, and K. Kompoliti, "TikTok Tics: A Pandemic within a Pandemic," *Movement Disorders Clinical Practice* 8, no. 8 (2021): 1200–1205, doi.org/10.1002/mdc3.13316. Christine Conelea and Clay Jones, "Don't Jump to Conclusions about So-Called TikTok Tics," Science-Based Medicine, Oct. 29, 2021, https://sciencebasedmedicine.org/dont-jump-to-conclusions-about-so-called-tiktok-tics/.

111 M. D. Manzar, A. Albougami, N. Usman, and M. A. Mamun, "Suicide among Adolescents and Youths during the COVID-19 Pandemic Lockdowns: A Press Media Reports-Based Exploratory Study," *Journal of Child and Adolescent Psychiatric Nursing* 34, no. 2 (2021): 139–46, https://doi.org/10.1111/jcap.12313:

"**Methods:** A purposive sampling of Google news between 15 February and 6 July was performed. After excluding duplicate reports, the final list comprised a total of 37-suicide cases across 11 countries.

Findings: More male suicides were reported (21-cases, i.e., 56.76%), and the mean age of the total victims was 16.6 ± 2.7 years (out of a total of 29 cases). About two-thirds of the suicides were from three countries named India (11-cases), UK (8-cases), and the USA (6-cases). Out of 23-student victims, 14 were school-going students. Hanging was the most common suicide method accounting in 51.4% of cases. The most common suicide causalities were related to mental sufferings such as depression, loneliness, psychological distress, and so forth, whereas either online schooling or overwhelming academic distress was placed as the second most suicide stressors followed by TikTok addiction-related psychological distress and tested with the COVID-19."

112 T. Molnar, "Technology, and the Ethical Imperative," *Chronicles*, February 1988, p. 14.

113 G. Steiner, *Real Presences* (Chicago, IL: University of Chicago Press, 1989).

114 J. Staddon, "The Devolution of Psychological Science: Memes, Culture, and Systematic Racism," *Academic Questions* 34, no. 3 (2021): 42–47. John P. A. Ioannidis, "How the Pandemic Is Changing the Norms of Science," *Tablet*, September 8, 2021, Tabletmag.com/sections/science/articles/pandemic-science; also, James Hankins, "Ten Things I Learned from the Pandemic," *First Things*, February 9, 2021. See also S. A. Klavan, "Worlds Without End," *Claremont Review of Books* 22, no. 3 (Summer 2022): 73.

115 Alex Berezow, "Why Are Medical Journals Full of Fashionable Nonsense?," *Big Think*, October 24, 2021, Bigthink.com/health/medical-journals-fashionable-nonsense; Berezow quotes from Alan Sokal and Jean Bricmont *Fashionable Nonsense: Postmodern Intellectuals' Abuse of Science* (New York, NY: Picador, 1999). See also Mahoney, D. J., "Pierre Manent and the New French Thought," *Crisis*, January 1995, 38–44. Also Cameron English, "Science Destroys Its Credibility by Embracing Critical Theory," Big Think, October 12, 2022, https://bigthink.com/health/critical-theory-science-destroys-credibility/.

116 B.-C. Han, *Non-things* (Cambridge: Polity Press, 2022), 6.

117 John J. Conley, "Who's Afraid of Transhumanism? (We All Should Be)," *America*, September 5, 2017, https://www.americamagazine.org/politics-society/2017/09/05/whos-afraid-transhumanism-we-all-should-be.

118 Ray Kurzweil, *The Singularity Is Near: When Humans Transcend Biology* (New York: Penguin, 2005). James Tunney, *Human Entrance to Transhumanism: Machine Merger and the End of Humanity* (self-pub, 2021).

119 Conley, "Who's Afraid of Transhumanism?," 1.

120 Claude Shannon, interview, *Omni*, August 1987, p. 32.

121 Samuel Gibbs, "Apple Co-founder Steve Wozniak Says Humans Will Become Robots' Pets," The Guardian, June 25, 2015, https://www.theguardian.com/technology/2015/jun/25/apple-co-founder-steve-wozniak-says-humans-will-be-robots-pets.

122 L. Kutz, "Gnosticism" (unpublished paper, 2005), available from author, P.C.V.; also see Ioan P. Couliano, in his *The Tree of Gnosis: Gnostic Mythology from Early Christianity to Modern Nihilism* (San Francisco: Harper Collins, 1992); also see Conley, "Who's Afraid of Transhumanism?"

123 See Kenneth Samples, "Heresies Never Die: Gnosticism," *Reflections* (blog), *Reasons to Believe*, February 14, 2023, https://reasons.org/explore/blogs/reflections/heresies-never-die-gnosticism. Also see Philip Jenkins, "The Heresy That Wouldn't Die," *Christian History*, 2007, no. 96, available online at https://christianhistoryinstitute.org/magazine/article/the-heresy-that-wouldn-t-die. Bishop Barron also discussed Gnosticism on his *Word on Fire Show*, March 9, 2020, available on YouTube at https://www.youtube.com/watch?v=JOvVgqBpeTY.

124 "By the turn of the century, however, as illustrated by the *Catholic Encyclopedia* article of 1913, principal orthodox Catholic scholars, along with most other scholars, had concluded that 'The first traces of Gnostic systems can be discerned some centuries before the Christian era.' This conclusion has been greatly reinforced and more narrowly defined by recent scholarship facilitated by the striking 1945 'Nag Hammadi' (Egypt) find of some new second and third centuries' AD tractates, the majority of which have been judged to be 'Gnostic'; many make no reference to Christianity, but rather reference, oppose, and deform Old Testament teaching, thus strongly indicating the origins of Gnosticism in radical intellectual and spiritual rebellion within or on the fringes of Jewish thought and life before Christ." L. Kutz, "Gnosticism and the Digital World" (unpublished manuscript, 2020), pp. 1–2.

125 "Perhaps the most significant aspect of Gnosticism as it relates historically to the life—individual and collective—of humanity… is its ruthless attack on human sexuality… Under analysis, however, the objective seems to have been the especially diabolical one of inducing human beings not to have children… so that God's plan for creation to populate the earth in order that heaven might finally be filled would be undone…. Sex is seen as an evil (rather, what is considered evil is specifically sex that makes possible a child), and the female role in bearing new spirits imprisoned in bodies is especially deprecated" (John P. Meier, *A Marginal Jew—Rethinking the Historical Jesus*, Vol. I). Kutz, 2005, p. 4.

126 Kutz, 2005, pp. 8–9.

127 Kutz, 2005, p. 4.

128 Kutz, 2020: "A Gnostic scholar, Ioan P. Couliano, in his *The Tree of Gnosis* (1992), says that for Marcion the greatest tragedy was not the creation of this world but the creation of mankind, made by the Demiurge in his image, out of low-quality materials—that 'fleshed stuff with excrement….,'" p. 5.

129 "*The Gospel of Thomas* [The Nag Hammadi Library, Codex II.2. 114] finishes with this lapidary verdict … 'Simon Peter said to them, 'Let Mary leave us, for women are not worthy of life.' Jesus said, 'I myself shall lead her in order

to make her male, so that she too may become a living spirit resembling you males. For every woman who will make herself male will enter the kingdom of heaven." Giovanni. Filoramo, *A History of Gnosticism,* trans. Anthony Alcock (Oxford: Basil Blackwell, 1990), 177), quoted in Kutz 2005, p. 6.

130 "The heart of the spirit found [in Gnosticism] might most properly be called 'militant pantheistic atheism.' Unlike any of the other authors and movements of that time or before and therefore defining Gnosticism itself, is a unique ruthlessness... in attacking the truth about God, man and the world, especially as it is revealed in the Old Testament, and this in the name of an unknown god and the highest spirituality." Kutz, 2005, p. 2.

131 The internet has many references to the dangers of AI. See for example, Mike Thomas, "12 Risks and Dangers of Artificial Intelligence (AI)," March 1, 2024, Built In, https://builtin.com/artificial-intelligence/risks-of-artificial-intelligence.

132 See Roger Scruton, *Beauty* (Oxford: Oxford University Press, 2009); Roger Scruton, *Modern Philosophy: An Introduction and Survey* (Oxford: Bloomsbury Reader, 1994). Caroline Walker Bynum makes a supporting case, in *Dissimilar Similitudes: Devotional Objects in Late Medieval Europe* (Princeton, NJ: Princeton University Press, 2020), that we should concentrate on the "thingness" of objects in order to see their true natures.

133 David Sax, *The Revenge of Analog: Real Things and Why They Matter* (New York, NY: Public Affairs, 2017). David Sax, *The Future of Analog: How to Create a More Human World* (New York, NY: Public Affairs, 2022).

134 Robert Pirsig, *Zen and the Art of Motorcycle Maintenance* (New York: HarperCollins, 1974).

135 R. Sennett, *The Craftsman* (New Haven, CT: Yale University Press, 2008).

136 Matthew Crawford, *Shop Class as SoulCraft* (New York: Penguin, 2009). The British edition (London: Penguin Books Ltd., 2009) is titled *The Case for Working with Your Hands, or Why Office Work Is Bad for Us and Fixing Things Feels Good.*

137 P. Korn, *Why We Make Things and Why It Matters: The Education of a Craftsman* (Boston, MA: D. R. Godine, 2013).

138 E. Gorges, *A Craftsman's Legacy: Why Working with Our Hands Gives Us Meaning* (Chapel Hill, NC: Algonquin, 2019). Also, S. Corbett, and S. Housley, "The Craftivist Collective Guide to Craftivism," *Utopian Studies* 22, no. 2 (2011): 344–51.

139 C. Tudge, *Six Steps Back to the Land* (Cambridge: Green Books, 2016).

140 C. Smaje, *A Small Farm Future* (White River Junction, VT: Chelsea Green, 2020).

141 Wendell Berry, *The Unsettling of America* (San Francisco, CA: Sierra Club Books, 1977); Wendell Berry, *Life Is a Miracle: An Essay Against Modern Superstition* (Berkeley, CA: Counterpoint, 2001); Wendell Berry, *The World-End-*

ing Fire: The Essential Wendell Berry, selected and with an introduction by Paul Kingsnorth (Berkeley, CA: Counterpoint Press, 2017).

142 See K. Mudge and S. Gabriel, *Farming the Woods: An Integrated Permaculture Approach to Growing Food and Medicinals in Temperate Forests* (White River Junction, VT: Chelsea Green, 2014); G. Kleppel, *The Emergent Agriculture: Farming, Sustainability, and the Return of the Local Economy* (Gabriola Island, BC: New Society, 2014); H. A. Okvat and A. J. Zautra, "Community Gardening: A Parsimonious Path to Individual, and Environmental Resilience," *Community Psychology* 47, no. 3-4 (2011): 374–87. Also, Abigail Gehring, ed., *Back to Basics: A Complete Guide to Traditional Skills* (New York: Skyhorse, 2014); and Carla Emery, *The Encyclopedia of Country Living, 50th Anniversary Edition: The Original Manual for Living off the Land & Doing It Yourself* (Seattle: Sasquatch Books, 2019). Also see Tobias J. Lanz, ed., *Beyond Capitalism & Socialism: A New Statement of an Old Ideal* (Norfolk, VA: IHS Press, 2008); A. Carlson, "The Case for Christian Distributism: The Authentic American Way," *Chronicles* 44, no. 7 (July 2020): 14–16.

143 G. Carrus, M. Scopelliti, R. Lafortezza, G. Colangelo, F. Ferrini, F. Salbitano, et al., "Go Greener, Feel Better? The Positive Effects of Biodiversity on the Well-Being of Individuals Visiting Urban and Peri-Urban Green Areas," *Landscape and Urban Planning* 134 (2015): 221–28.

144 M. G. Berman, J. Jonides, and S. Kaplan, "The Cognitive Benefits of Interacting with Nature," *Psychological Science* 19, no. 12 (2008):1207–12; Y. Tsunetsugu, B. Park, and Y. Miyazaki, "Trends in Research Related to 'Shinrin-yoku' (Taking in the Forest Atmosphere, or Forest Bathing) in Japan," *Environmental Health and Preventive Medicine* 15, no. 1 (2010): 27.

145 S. Kesebir and P. Kesebir, "A Growing Disconnection from Nature Evident in Cultural Products," *Perspectives on Psychological* Science 12, no. 2 (2017): 258–69.

146 R. Dreher, *The Benedict Option. A Strategy for Christians in a Post-Christian Nation* (New York, NY: Sentinel, 2017).

147 Brett and Kate McKay, "Communities vs. Networks: To Which Do You Belong?," Art of Manliness, July 1, 2014, https://www.artofmanliness.com/people/relationships/communities-vs-networks-to-which-do-you-belong/).

148 Stacy Jones, "Computers and Technology in Montessori Schools," Montessori For Today, June 23, 2024, https://montessorifortoday.com/computers-and-technology-in-montessori-schools/. Chloë Marshall, "Montessori Education: A Review of the Evidence Base," *NPJ Science of Learning* 2, no. 11 (2017). doi: 10.1038/s41539-017-0012-7.

149 J. Cobb, *Prepper's Long-Term Survival Guide: Food, Shelter, Security, Off-the-Grid Power and More Life-Saving Strategies for Self-Sufficient Living* (Berkeley, CA: Ulysses Press, 2020).

150 Nick Arama, "New poll shows large number on both sides of aisle favor seceding into 'Red/Blue' states," Red State, October 1, 2021, Redstate.com/nick.arama/2021/10/01/new-poll-shows-large-number-on-both-sides-of-aisle-favor-seceding-into-red-blue-states-n450924.

151 T. J. Kaczynski, *Technological Slavery*, vol. 1, revised and expanded edition (Scottsdale, AZ: Fitch & Madison, 2019), 257.

152 R. Kurzweil, *The Singularity is Near* (London: Penguin Books, 2005).

153 Kaczynski, *Technological Slavery*, pp. 5–7, 196.

154 Quoted by L. M. Sacasas in "From Common Sense to Bespoke Realities," *The Convivial Society* 3, no. 12, https://theconvivialsociety.substack.com/p/from-common-sense-to-bespoke-realities.

155 Bronze Age Pervert, *Bronze Age Mindset* (self-pub, 2018).

156 Integral calculus involves digital procedures for evaluating area under curves for which you have the digital formulae. Area is a high-level analog notion that in scientific usage commonly involves concrete area. In addition, the derivative of a function is its slope at a given point, and again digital procedures allow the evaluation of the slope, which itself is an analog property.

157 T. Wolfe, *The Painted Word* (New York: Farrar, Straus & Giroux, 1975).

158 José Ortega y Gasset, "The Dehumanization of Art," in *The Dehumanization of Art and Other Essays on Art, Culture, and Literature* (Princeton, NJ: Princeton University Press, 1968); see also Oliver Holmes, "José Ortega y Gasset," *The Stanford Encyclopedia of Philosophy*, Summer 2022 Edition, ed. Edward N. Zalta, https://plato.stanford.edu/archives/sum2022/entries/gasset/.

159 References re contemporary realist painters of beauty. Names to include: Andrew Wyeth, Fairfield Porter, Jane Wilson, Philip Pearlstein, Alex Katz, Jack Beal, Neil Welliver, Roberto Ferri, Jeremy Lipkin, Francis O'Toole, Stephen Bauman, Conor Walton, Mario Robinson, Jesús Meneses del Barco.

160 Paul Johnson, *Intellectuals* (New York: Harper & Row, 1988); Roger Scruton, *Fools, Frauds, and Firebrands: Thinkers of the New Left* (London: Bloomsbury, 2015).

161 H. Elberg-Schwartz, ed., *People of the Body: Jews and Judaism from an Embodied Perspective* (Albany: State University of New York Press, 1992).